THE ESSEX LIBRARY

Essex Eccentrics

Essex Eccentrics

ALISON BARNES

THE BOYDELL PRESS . IPSWICH

© 1975 Alison Barnes

Published by the Boydell Press Ltd
PO Box 24 Ipswich IP1 1JJ

First published 1975
ISBN 0 85115 058 6 (library)
0 85115 059 4 (paper)

Printed in Great Britain by
Dramrite Printers Limited,
Long Lane, Southwark, London SE1

To my mother

CONTENTS

Illustrations

INTRODUCTION

Few counties in England can claim more eccentrics than Essex. In the past its impenetrable forests, lonely marshlands and isolated villages were ideally suited to the flourishing of singularity and bred all sorts of odd characters. The people of Essex, always noted for their love of individualism, were proud of these characters and regarded even the most ridiculous with good-humoured tolerance. They appreciated the originality of their views and admired the spirited way in which they pursued their fantasies and flouted the conventions. Before the advent of pop-stars and television, of course, eccentrics were also highly prized as entertainers. Their outlandish clothes, hilarious exploits and racy quips added zest to dull rural existences and supplied wonderful material for gossip.

Since the Second World War, however, the face of Essex has changed. Its forests have become increasingly less secluded, much of its coast has been parcelled out into nature reserves or turned into yacht marinas, and villages once tiny and remote are now ringed about by housing estates and connected by motorways. In this bureaucratic environment there is little scope for individuality, and although a few bizarre characters may still be found in Essex, the days of the truly great eccentrics have, I feel, gone for ever.

My aim in writing this book has been to help keep alive the memory of some of the most striking of these personalities. And so as to give a satisfactory idea of the wide range of Essex eccentricity I have included figures of national importance as well as relative unknowns; characters who have been fully documented and those about whom only a few brief tantalising snippets can be gleaned. Some of the men and women portrayed were consistently odd for the greater part of their lives, others achieved renown by means of a single peculiar action. But each one has contributed something unique to the county's social history and deserves to be remembered.

Many people have given me information about my eccentrics and I am extremely grateful to them all, but I should like to thank in particular Mrs J. Boyden, Mr D. C. Bright, Mrs E. B. Carswell, Mr A. C. Edwards and Mr A. Kimble. For their courtesy and helpfulness I also wish to thank Mr John Turner and Miss Sheila Jordain of the Saffron Walden Museum and the staff of the Essex Record Office who gave much useful advice.

Glorious eccentrics! Every age is enlivened by their presence.

Aldous Huxley, *Crome Yellow*

Chapter One

THE MISERS OF ASHEN

One autumn day in 1735, John Meggot entered a quiet little Chelmsford hostelry, dressed in the height of fashion. He emerged, half an hour later, wearing a tattered coat, darned worsted stockings, and shoes done up with rusty iron buckles. The young man was on his way to visit his rich but miserly uncle, Sir Harvey Elwes, whose heir he was to be, and knowing that the old skinflint hated anyone to waste money on clothes, he assumed these rags so as to make a good impression on his relative.

In this he succeeded, for when he arrived at Stoke College, the Elwes' family seat on the Essex-Suffolk border, his uncle surveyed him with evident satisfaction and invited him to share his supper, which consisted of a partridge and a single boiled potato. After the meal uncle and nephew sat huddled over a dreary fire, with one glass of wine between them, and when it grew dark they retired to rest, for, as Sir Harvey was fond of saying, 'Going to bed saves candlelight.'

After this first visit John felt it his duty to spend several weeks a year with his uncle. He was a hearty eater and would not have survived long at Stoke if he hadn't dined secretly with friends before supping with Sir Harvey. By then, of course, his appetite was diminished, and the miser was delighted to see his nephew eat so sparingly.

Summer or winter, Sir Harvey always wore the same clothes; a full-dress suit, a moth-eaten greatcoat, and a ragged black cap pulled down over his eyes. In this trim he would ride about his estates, perched on a broken-winded old nag as gaunt and miserable as himself. John Meggot often accompanied him on these journeys, dressed in like scarecrow manner.

Small wonder, then, that the pair came to be christened 'The Misers of Ashen'. Sir Harvey owned much of the property and land around this little Essex village, and he and his nephew frequently stopped at his farm there, Claret Hall, in the hope of cadging a free meal from the tenant. At that time John had not yet earned the title of miser. He was a fast London dandy who spent his days whoring and gambling—only acting the miser when on a visit to his uncle. But, certainly, the title was well bestowed on Sir Harvey.

He first acquired habits of economy when, on inheriting the family estates from his grandfather, Sir Jervaise, he found that numerous debts had been left unpaid. By diligent pinching and scraping he soon rid himself of creditors, but he could not get rid of his mania for economising. Indeed, he carried this policy of saving to such ludicrous extremes that, although possessed of £250,000, for several years before his death his annual expenditure was only £100.

From birth Sir Harvey had been puny. He grew up shy and taciturn and managed to pass through school, college and a long parliamentary career without making a single friend. So he retired to his mansion at Stoke-by-Clare, where he could follow the only pursuits that interested him—hoarding gold and partridge setting.

He lived almost entirely on partridges and insisted that his manservant and two maids should do likewise. Every day during the season he would be up betimes, stalking the woods and fields until nightfall. Game was so plentiful on the estates and Sir Harvey such a good shot that he often took five or six hundred brace of birds in one winter. If he wanted an occasional change of diet he would catch the fish in his ponds or use some of the milk produced by his cows, though this was usually sold to neighbouring farmers. His woods supplied all the fuel that was needed, but even in this commodity Sir Harvey felt he had to economise. If his nephew or a tenant came to see him, he would put one stick in the grate and would not light another until it had nearly burnt through. He never had a fire when he was alone, but would pace briskly up and down the hall to keep warm.

To have bought new clothes would have seemed wilful extravagance to the miser, for wasn't there a chest upstairs full of the mouldering garb of his ancestors? When one suit was wearing thin, he unlocked this box and took out another—often in the style of fifty or a hundred years back.

Although he invested most of his capital, Sir Harvey liked to have part of his gold with him in the house. And eventually a notorious band of thieves, known as the Thaxted gang, got wind of this and came to rob him. Making a surprise attack late at night, the thieves bound and gagged Sir Harvey's servants and then rushed up to his room and, holding pistols to his head, demanded his money. Seeing that the men were not to be trifled with, the miser pointed to the trunk containing his hoard and watched in anguish as they loaded the two thousand seven hundred guineas into baskets and then made off.

A few years later the robbers were caught in Chelmsford, and Sir Harvey's lawyer urged him to go and identify them. But he would not hear of it. 'No, no', he said, 'I have lost my money, and now you want me to lose my time also.'

This parsimonious old gentleman died in 1763, at the age of eighty-seven. In his will he left his entire fortune to John Meggot, stipulating that he assume the name and arms of Elwes.

The house at Stoke was in shocking condition when Mr Elwes inherited it. Windows were cracked, paint was peeling off the walls and dust lay thick upon the furniture. In the bedrooms the ancient canopies were festooned with cobwebs and full of gaping moth holes. In fact the place perfectly verified a local saying that 'nobody would live with Sir Harvey Elwes if they could, nor could if they would'.

As has already been mentioned, in his youth John Elwes was something of a rake. His father, Robert Meggot, descendant of the famous Dean Meggot of Winchester, was a wealthy London brewer, and when he died in 1718, he left his four-year-old son well supplied with money.

After completing his education at Westminster School John was sent to Geneva for three years, and he soon became the star pupil of the riding academy there. He was totally fearless and delighted in performing feats of daring such as jumping his horse over high walls, or galloping about on wild, untamed ponies.

When he returned to England the young man plunged straight into the gaieties of society life. He dressed like a swell, rode in Hyde Park with pretty girls and joined all the best gambling clubs of the day. Once he played for thirty-six hours without stopping, and at the end of the session he and his companions found themselves knee-deep in used cards.

During the next twenty years Mr Elwes divided his time between London, Stoke and his country seat at Marcham in Berkshire, where he had two illegitimate sons by the housekeeper, Elizabeth Moren.

Traits of miserliness began to appear in Elwes as he grew older. These he inherited partly from his uncle and partly from his mother, who starved herself to death although her husband had left her £100,000. By the time he moved to Stoke College, at the age of fifty, Mr Elwes was an even greater miser than Sir Harvey had been, but a miser of a completely different stamp. For he was gay and witty and, apart from his really staggering economies, knew how to enjoy life. Only in his dotage did his love of gold deteriorate into the obsession that finally bore him to the grave.

When his uncle's house had been made habitable Mr Elwes ordered a kennel block to be added, and as soon as it was ready he filled it with some of the best hunting dogs in England. These animals were the darlings of his heart and lived lives of pampered luxury. Not so his huntsman. In the morning this harassed individual was expected to milk the cows, prepare breakfast for Mr Elwes and his guests, feed the hounds and saddle the horses. He then had to ride hard all day. At night he fed all the animals, groomed the horses, cooked supper and waited at table. And his only reward was to be called an 'idle dog' by his master.

Mr Elwes loved to be on horseback, and when he wasn't hunting he would ride round his estates at Ashen and Ridgewell, go to Newmarket to watch the races, or gallop down to London. Even on the longest journeys he never stopped at an inn but took provisions with him in his greatcoat pockets. Two hard-boiled eggs might be all he would eat during a whole day, and if he wanted a drink he would halt by a stream and refresh himself and his mount at the same time.

Once when Mr Elwes went to Newmarket with his friend, Mr Spurling, of Dynes Hall, Great Maplestead, he forgot about food altogether. Mr Spurling grew hungrier and hungrier but didn't like to say anything until, quite desperate, on the homeward journey he suggested they call at an inn. 'No need for that, my dear fellow', Elwes replied, and producing a mouldy pancake from his pocket, offered his friend half of it. He then casually mentioned that he had brought the pancake from Marcham two months before, and added that he was glad to see it was 'as good as new'.

On another occasion when Mr Elwes was returning from Newmarket with Mr Spurling, his friend was riding a little ahead and was about to go through the turnpike by Devil's Ditch when he heard Elwes halloo and went back to him without paying. 'Here, here, come with me, this is the best road', Elwes said. And next moment he was urging his horse up the near-perpendicular slope of the ditch. Heart in mouth Mr Spurling followed, and after great difficulty the two men reached the other side. Mr Spurling wiped

4

John Elwes Esq.ᴿ

1. John Elwes, the celebrated miser.

the sweat from his brow and thanked God for their safe deliverance. 'Aye', said Mr Elwes, 'you mean from the turnpike. Very right. Never pay a turnpike if you can avoid it.'

Paying doctors' bills was another thing Elwes avoided whenever possible. He would not allow his sons to receive medical attention, and if he injured himself out hunting he would wait until the wound turned gangrenous before summoning aid. On one occasion when he was staying in London with his nephew, Richard Timms, a colonel in the Horse Guards, Mr Elwes cut both his legs by running into the poles of a sedan chair. His nephew insisted that he see a doctor, but after the physician had made his examination Elwes said to him: 'In my opinion my legs are not much hurt. Now you think they are, so I will make this agreement: I will take one leg and you shall take the other; you shall do what you please with yours, and I will do nothing with mine, and I wager your bill that my leg gets well the first'. It did!

In 1772, when he was fifty-eight, Mr Elwes decided to stand for election as M.P. for Berkshire. So he left Stoke and went to Marcham to help canvass. Costly dinners for his supporters were, of course, out of the question. But Mr Elwes did very nicely by making witty speeches and attending the dances given in his honour. At these assemblies he made a point of 'tripping it' with as many ladies as he could, and he leapt and twirled in so sprightly a manner that he won general admiration—and the votes that gave him his seat.

Mr Elwes remained in Parliament for twelve years. He always did his best for his constituents and supported the measures that he felt would benefit them most, regardless of party loyalties. This conduct led to his being nicknamed 'The Parliamentary Coquette'.

From his father, Mr Elwes had inherited property round the Haymarket, and he himself built large parts of Marylebone and Portman Square. All these houses he let to wealthy tenants, but there were usually two or three standing empty at any given time, and in one or other of these he lived when in London. A couple of beds, two chairs, a table and an old charwoman made up his furniture, and this he moved from house to house as the one he was in got taken. Elwes never bothered to insure his property, saying that he did not mind running risks. And, indeed, on one occasion when he learnt that a particularly fine house of his had been burnt to the ground, his only comment was a cool, 'Well, well, there is no great harm done. The tenant never paid me, and I should not have got quit of him so quickly in any other way.'

During his years in Parliament Mr Elwes lived a life of extraordinary contrast. When at home, he supped with his housekeeper off tripe and onions. But if his friends invited him out he would dine sumptuously at their expense and prove to be a connoisseur of French wines and cookery. He kept no manservant in London and always dressed like a pauper even when attending Parliament. So wretched did he look in fact that people would stop him in the street and give him alms. Yet when he was presented at Court, he outshone dukes and earls with his finery. Mr Elwes could never bring himself to part with a shilling for a cab but was to be seen trudging round London in all weathers. Sometimes his parliamentary friends took pity on him and invited him into their carriages, and then he was glad enough of the ride.

In 1784 the coalition between Fox and Lord North collapsed, and Elwes resigned from Parliament and again went to live at Stoke College. When he reached the house he was horrified to discover that his youngest son, John, had actually spent money refurnishing some of the rooms. He soon put a stop to this kind of nonsense, however, and embarked on a course of rigid economy. In winter he sat in the kitchen with the servants to save fire and in summer he went gleaning at Claret Hall. So as to avoid buying horseshoes Mr Elwes rode his mare on grass alone. He would not allow his own shoes to be cleaned in case the rubbing wore them out. For clothes this old miser now resorted to Sir Harvey's chest, and many a weird garment did he pull from it. On one occasion when his friend and biographer, Captain Edward Topham, was staying with him, Mr Elwes appeared at dinner wearing riding boots, a green Elizabethan jacket with slashed sleeves and the foul-smelling wig of a beggar that he had picked out of a ditch. The wig was jet-black and contrasted strangely with his own white hair, which straggled down beneath it.

When entertaining visitors Mr Elwes provided fresh game from his park. But if he was alone he often ate meat so full of maggots that it walked about his plate. He once supped off the remains of a moorhen that had been gnawed by a rat, and (crowning economy of his life) on another occasion he fished up a pike that contained a second, undigested pike in its stomach. 'Ah', chortled Elwes in huge delight, 'this is really killing two birds with one stone!'

Despite his increasing passion for economy, at seventy-three Mr Elwes had not lost his sense of humour. One day he was out shooting in a wood near Ridgewell with Captain Topham and another friend when the third man, who was a very poor shot, lodged two pellets in Mr Elwes's cheek. The wound bled profusely and Elwes was in great pain, but when the man came up to apologise, he said with a laugh, 'My dear sir, I give you joy on your improvement—I knew you would hit something by and by.'

After spending three years at Stoke Mr Elwes moved to Theydon Hall, his damp and dismal farmhouse on the borders of Epping Forest. The tenants, an elderly couple who kept very much to their own part of the house, were the only people he saw for weeks on end, and when John Timms, his grand-nephew, did eventually come to visit him, he found the old man lying ill and half-starved in his room. Apparently the miser had refused to allow a doctor to be called, for fear of the expense, and had forbidden his tenants to buy him the delicacies necessary to tempt his appetite.

Mr Timms took his uncle to London and nursed him back to health. As soon as he recovered Elwes made his will, and in it he left his property to his grand-nephew and £150,000 to each of his sons.

In 1788 Mr Elwes spent the summer at his house in Welbeck Street, and it was here that he had his last romance. At the age of seventy-four he fell desperately in love with the kitchenmaid, and would have married her, too, if his son, George, hadn't swooped down in the nick of time and borne him off to Marcham.

Mr Elwes took nothing with him to Berkshire except five guineas and a half and half-a-crown. This small treasure he guarded as jealously as if it had been his whole fortune, and he hid it in a different cache every hour.

One night a Mr Partis, who was staying at Marcham, heard someone padding about in his room. 'Who is there?' he called, rather frightened.

'Sir', said the intruder, coming up to his bed, 'my name is Elwes. I have been unfortunate enough to be robbed in this house, which I believe is mine, of all the money I have in the world, of five guineas and a half and half-a-crown.'

'Dear sir', replied Mr Partis, 'I hope you are mistaken; pray do not make yourself uneasy.'

'Oh, no, no!' cried Elwes, wringing his hands, 'it is too true.'

The money was found next day, hidden behind a window shutter.

For two or three months before his death the fear of losing this bit of gold so preyed on Mr Elwes's mind that he could hardly eat or sleep for worry. Finally he grew so weak that he had to be put to bed, and once there he fell into a semi-coma, muttering end-

8

lessly to himself, 'My money! My money! Where is my money?'

Seeing that his father had not long to live, George sent for John. And on the morning of the 26th November, 1789, the brothers were sitting by Mr Elwes's bedside when his grip on John's hand suddenly relaxed; his fretful muttering ceased—the great god Mammon had claimed his own.

Chapter Two

TRAMPS AND HERMITS

The most eccentric tramps in Essex at the turn of the century were Marmalade Emma and Teddy Grimes, a pair of vagrants who travelled the roads in the Colchester area up until the First World War. Their appearance in itself was startling. Teddy had matted grey hair, a drooping moustache, gold rings in his ears. He wore two or three coats, one on top of the other. Often one of his boots would be black, one brown. He always carried a large sack over his shoulder. Emma would be attired in some cast-off, flouncy Victorian dress, over which she wore a thick tweed jacket. Inside this jacket lived her cat, and every now and then its head would poke out at the top as it came up for air. Pots and pans dangled from a rope fastened to Emma's waist. She sometimes carried a neatly furled umbrella. But her crowning glories were the vast straw hats, lavishly bedecked with roses, ribbons and ostrich feathers, that she affected during the summer months.

Marmalade Emma (so called because of her great fondness for this preserve) and Grimes were not married but, despite frequent tiffs, they remained devoted to each other. Where the couple originated from, or what their past lives had been, no one ever discovered. When they first appeared around Colchester they spent their days going from house to house begging for food and their nights sleeping in ditches or under haystacks. Even in winter, when a snug barn was sometimes offered them as a sleeping-place, they preferred to stay out in the open. And once during a snow-storm a traveller on the Mersea road came upon the pair crouched over a cheerless fire; Emma nonchalantly smoking her short clay pipe, Grimes reading a newspaper.

Not surprisingly Emma developed bronchial troubles, and in the end she and Grimes went to live on a derelict barge on the Colne. They still tramped about begging for food, however, and on one of these excursions Emma used foul language to a policeman and was put in gaol. When she came out the Colchester street urchins asked her where she had been, and she replied primly, 'To college.'

Emma adored the cat that she carried about with her and always gave it the choicest morsels she and Teddy collected. On one occasion when she had to go to the Essex County Hospital, she managed to smuggle the creature into the ward. Later a nurse discovered the cat and tried to take it from her. Emma screamed and fought desperately to keep the animal, but it was removed and placed in a shed.

Marmalade Emma eventually died on board the barge. Grimes followed her to the grave within a few months, and they were buried side by side in a Colchester cemetery.

In the 1880s another curious pair of tramps had trudged the byways around Colchester. They were known as the 'Silly Hannahs' and were thought to be sisters. Like Emma and Grimes they slept rough, but they earned money for their food by selling mats and baskets that they made out of rushes. The eldest sister believed she was a queen and always walked a little in front of the younger, balancing an extraordinary pile of hats on her head. When they knocked at the door of a house to sell their wares the 'queen' would ask for another hat to add to her collection, and if she was given one, she would jam it down on top of the others and vouchsafe the donor a regal nod of thanks.

During the latter half of the sixteenth century, when a man needed a passport to travel from one parish to the next and a licence to open any sort of shop or ale-house, two vagabonds, Dave Bennett and Tom Whiting, did a roaring trade in counterfeit documents. Taking separate routes they walked from one end of Essex to the other, stopping at the towns and villages where they thought their services might be required. They met every few months at a certain house near Ugley Hall to report progress and share their earnings.

Dave, who had a face 'full of pockeholes', travelled about with a buxom wench called Mary Philips, by whom he had an illegitimate child. He muffled himself up in a long black cloak. Tom favoured even more exotic garb and at all times wore 'a white wolen night capte with two eares'. He carried a piece of chalk with him wherever he went and drew little whitings on tree-trunks and ale-house walls so that people would know which way to go if they wanted to find him.

For several years this pair of tramps puzzled Essex magistrates, who could not understand why so many men held licences that they did not remember signing. The couple were eventually caught and imprisoned in December, 1581, when an old client informed against them.

A solitary tramp who wandered from village to village in the Epping district at the beginning of this century was William Foster, better known at 'Torp-Torp'. Attired in full hunting regalia he would walk along muttering to himself and occasionally shouting out, 'Torp torp torpee', hence the nickname. Mr Foster had once worked as a tailor, living with his sisters in a house in Epping called Rookwood. When his sisters died, William took to the road and led a hand-to-mouth existence which unbalanced him. He ended his days in the workhouse.

Another lone tramp was Ardleigh Ben, who originated from the village whose name he bore. During the summer he travelled about the Essex countryside, playing an imaginary fiddle and singing accompaniments. He would sometimes stop and give performances on village greens, when he would dance and act the clown as well as sing. These antics earned him enough money to pay for food and the occasional night's lodging at an inn.

When autumn drew to a close Ben would make his way back to the Tendring workhouse, where he was in the habit of spending the winter. The workhouse staff disliked Ben because he was lazy and shirked his duties, and one winter in the 1870s they pretended that there was no room for him in the house. The old man begged them to take him in, saying that he would sleep anywhere. When he heard this the workhouse master thought that he would teach Ben a lesson, so he told him he could stay—provided he slept in the mortuary. The tramp agreed and was taken down into the dismal chamber, where a corpse already reposed. As soon as the workhouse master had gone, Ben lifted the cadaver out of its coffin, propped it up by the door and then curled up in the coffin and went to sleep.

Next morning the master came in to see how Ben had fared and was almost startled out of his wits when the corpse fell against him and a lugubrious voice from the coffin said, 'These be hard times, master.' The tramp was given a comfortable bed in the workhouse from that time onwards.

One evening in the early 1920s, a well-dressed tramp entered the bar of the old 'Fox' inn at Hatfield Broad Oak and ordered a pint of beer. He smiled at the company and announced, 'My name is Sammy Lavender.' Intrigued by this the regulars began to talk to the tramp and they soon discovered that he was no ordinary vagabond, for he claimed to have seen angels and to have conversed with them frequently.

At closing time the landlady, Mrs Patmore, allowed Sammy to spend the night in the loft above her stable. And he found it so snug and convenient that he remained there for several years. Sometimes he would do a little work in the fields, and this paid for his beer and tobacco. For food he relied on the generosity of the villagers.

One lunch-time Sammy ran into the 'Fox' in a very excited state and cried, 'I'm agoin' to die next Saturday night at twelve o'clock. A angel came out of the clouds and told me so.'

Everyone laughed, but on the Saturday evening a number of people followed the tramp to bed to see what would happen. It was somewhat eerie in the loft, with the wind shrieking through the rafters and fitful shadows dancing on the walls. Sammy lay on his bed surrounded by villagers. A man with a watch sat by the candle. No one spoke. Suddenly the tramp began to gasp and moan. He writhed about as if in agony.

'Two minutes to twelve', whispered the time-keeper.

The gasping noises intensified. Then a clock struck midnight. Sammy gurgled in his throat and lay still.

'He's gone', a woman said in an awed voice.

But her more sceptical husband decided to 'test for it'. Taking a needle from his pocket he thrust it into Sammy's leg. 'Oh! Oh! Stop it!' yelped the tramp, springing up at once.

His trickery was revealed, and the villagers, furious at having been gulled, went for him tooth and nail. Then they locked the door of the loft and left him there for a whole day as a punishment. After that he was forgiven. But never again was talk at the 'Fox' enlivened by the sayings of angels.

In July, 1880, a mysterious tramp-cum-hermit pitched his tent on the edge of Hainault Forest at Chigwell. He had a black beard and kind grey eyes, and he told the local people that he would cure their ailments with his herbal remedies. He said that he was called Dido, but refused to give his real name or to talk about his past.

The tramp was neatly dressed, spoke in a cultured voice and appeared to be a man of great learning, and soon the whole Chigwell area was buzzing with rumours about his origin. Some folks had it that he belonged to a wealthy family and had been a medical student; others believed that he had once worked in a London shipping office, but all were agreed in thinking that he had had an unhappy love-affair and that, inconsolable as Queen Dido, he had adopted her name and sought refuge in the forest.

Whatever the truth of these rumours, one thing was certain: the tramp's herbal medicines were extremely effective in curing such ills as measles, whooping-cough, backache, liver troubles, bruises and sprains. His most famous remedy was a green ointment made from ferns. One winter the driver of the horse-drawn bus that ran daily from Lambourne to Woodford had such bad chilblains that he could not hold the reins. Dido applied the ointment to the man's fingers and bound each one separately. When the bandages were taken off a few days later the driver's hands were completely healed and he was able to return to work.

Dido had such confidence in the preventive qualities of his herbs that he would tend patients suffering from scarlet fever or diphtheria. Often he was the only person who would approach the stricken families, and his visits were a real comfort to them. As well as supplying medicines Dido would buy food for his patients, cook meals for them and tackle household chores.

When the London County Council took over Hainault Forest, Dido moved to Chigwell Row and camped for many years in a field in Vicarage Lane. He frequently left his tent to go foraging for herbs in the nearby countryside, and on these occasions he slept out in the open. When he returned he would brew his herbal mixtures over a low fire, cork them up in bottles and jars and set out again to sell his wares.

Dido sold 'tea' as well as medicines. The crafty old man used to pick sloe and hawthorn leaves, dry them, pound them up in a mortar and offer them to London tea merchants. 'You don't realise what you're taking when you drink China tea', he would tell his friends with a roguish chuckle.

In London Dido also sold songbirds in wicker cages, and even when very old he thought nothing of tramping from Chigwell to Bunhill Row and back in a day. 'Dido can do it', he used to say, 'he can beat the young uns yet.'

But no one goes tramping on for ever, and in 1902 the hermit died. It was then discovered that his real name was William Bell and that before he came to Hainault he had worked as a docker and part-time fishmonger in the East End. An aura of mystery still clings to him, however, and we shall probably never know exactly why he called himself Dido, or for what reason he decided to give up his job as a docker and lead a solitary life in the forest.

On Greyhound Common, Brentwood, in the early 1900s, there

14

lived a hermit known as 'Ole Oddy'. His flimsy shelter made of branches and sacking was furnished with a bed and some upturned pails which served as tables and chairs. He cooked his food outside on an open fire. When tending the fire or sitting in his hut 'Oddy' would be in what he called 'undress'. In this state he wore a pair of corduroy trousers, a grimy shirt, a red and white spotted handkerchief, a felt hat and a magnificent moleskin waistcoat, which grew from year to year as he caught additional moles and sewed their skins round the bottom. If he was going further afield, however, he donned a voluminous greatcoat with pockets reaching from waist to ground.

Every Saturday morning 'Oddy' came into the 'Brewery Tap' inn at Brentwood to drink his quart of ale and have a quiet smoke. He always smoked his pipe upside down. Halfway through the drink the hermit would suddenly put his hand into one of his pockets and pull out a rabbit, which he would sell for sixpence. And then, conjurer-like, he would go on pulling out rabbit after rabbit until twelve or more had been disposed of and his pockets were at last empty.

Charlie Haddock was another hermit who sold rabbits in a public house, the 'White Hart' in Harlow. He sometimes knocked on the back doors of favoured customers at midnight or later and offered them plump pheasants that he had illicitly shot with his catapult. He carried this catapult about with him everywhere and also a stout stick, with which he walloped the rabbits.

Charlie lived in the old gravel pit by the railway line at Harlow from 1935 to 1957. He had dug out a cave from the side of the pit and made for it a rough wooden door, which he painted garish colours. The cave was heated by a coal fire, fuel being supplied by local train drivers, who threw lumps of coal to Charlie as they hurtled past. It was lit by a foul-smelling lamp, which revealed Charlie's few possessions—a trunk, a bed and a rickety table. The walls of the cave were lined with £1 notes.

People often visited Charlie in his cave, and he would tell them how he had started life as a hermit soon after the First World War, when he built himself a tree-house in Epping Forest. Eventually he had been expelled from the forest by the keepers, and had then settled in Harlow. Before his visitors left, Charlie would show them the medals he had won during the war. He always gave children sixpence each as a parting gift. They were not at all afraid of the hermit, for with his deep kindly voice, twinkling blue eyes and white hair he appeared to them as a sort of grandfather figure.

Most of Charlie's income came from a mysterious allowance that he collected every month from a London solicitor. When he returned from the City there was always much jollification at the 'White Hart', where his friends were treated to round after round of free drinks. He was very popular at the inn, for he was not only generous, but amusing and could talk well on almost any subject.

Towards the end of his life Charlie caught pneumonia every winter and had to be taken to hospital. On one of these occasions, in 1957, vandals broke into his cave, stole most of his possessions and set fire to the remainder. When he came out of hospital the hermit went to live in a caravan on a farm near Sheering. He died in 1962 in a Colchester nursing home.

At the funeral an unknown woman appeared and claimed to be the hermit's sister, but she could not substantiate her claim and did not in any way resemble Charlie. Later a Mr Skate from Norfolk asserted that he was the hermit's brother. He did look very like Charlie, and it seemed typical of the dead man's sense of humour to abandon one fishy name (Skate) and take on another (Haddock).

From Mr Skate it was learnt that Charlie's father had been a farmer in Norfolk, and that after the old man's death Charlie had emigrated to Australia and bought a farm there. His family had not heard from him since those days, but it was believed that whilst in Australia he had become entangled with some girl and had fled to England under an assumed name. The hermit's war medals, which were examined by Mr Skate, were found not to have belonged to him at all. It was subsequently discovered that Mr Haddock had spent only six days in the Army.

Despite these revelations, people who knew Charlie speak of him with affection, for he brought a bit of excitement into their lives and provided them with a wealth of anecdotes to hand down to their children and grandchildren.

An even more spectacular fund of anecdotes was provided by Jimmy Mason for the people of Great Canfield. He was a real story-book hermit, complete with sackcloth, religious mania and a long white beard, and for many years he lived by himself in the middle of a wood. But he began life prosaically enough, being the eldest son of Richard Mason, a retired drill-sergeant who owned a house at Great Canfield called Sawkins. Mr Mason was a martinet and he tyrannised over Jimmy and his younger brother, Tommy, making them undergo all sorts of endurance tests and punishing them severely if they failed. Tommy took this treatment in his stride, but Jimmy was completely cowed by it. He became more and more neurotic until in 1873, when he was sixteen, he developed a phobia about being looked at (he was an exceedingly handsome boy) and determined to spend the rest of his life in seclusion.

So a hut was built for Jimmy in the orchard at Sawkins, and here he spent his days, spying on the neighbours with a telescope and listening to their conversations through the hedge. He was fond of children and as they came out of school he would throw them fruit, sweets and flowers. He never spoke to the youngsters and took care to keep well hidden, but he was pleased when they shouted out their thanks.

In 1890 Mr Mason died and Jimmy became head of the family. His father left him property and land in Great Canfield, so they were reasonably well-off. At about this time Jimmy began to hang presents for his girl friends on the railings in front of Sawkins. Sometimes he also hung gifts on the branches of fir trees or oak trees near the house. The gifts were put out after dark three or four times a week and varied from expensive trinkets to bags of apples or nuts. Money was occasionally given, carefully wrapped in tissue paper, and when he could think of nothing else Jimmy might leave out a cabbage or a cauliflower. Little notes would be fastened to each of the presents.

Fanny, Lizzie and Gertrude were the girls in Jimmy's life during the 1890s. Very little is known about Gertrude, but it appears that he first saw Fanny and Lizzie when they passed his hide in the orchard. Even when Lizzie was quite a child Jimmy sent her love-letters via his dog, tying the notes to its collar. She only saw him once, and then he told her that he worshipped her. In about 1891 Lizzie came to Sawkins as a maid, and Jimmy ogled her furtively from behind doors. When she walked in Hart Wood he hid in the bushes to watch her go by. This constant staring began to get on the poor girl's nerves, and in 1892 she left Great Canfield to become barmaid at the 'Fox', Hatfield Heath. Jimmy was heartbroken.

He soon consoled himself with Fanny, however, and by 1894, when she was fourteen, they were regularly exchanging notes and gifts on the railings. Fanny gave Jimmy the diary that he kept for several years, and he gave her many expensive presents, including a gold watch. She was apparently 'hot stuff', and Jimmy delighted in gazing at her well-developed figure, but he did not wish to be seen himself, so they only talked through the thick orchard hedge. Nothing came of this affair, for by 1896 Fanny had grown tired of Jimmy and was going out with boys of her own age. She left the village in 1897.

In 1906 Mrs Mason went into a nursing home, and Jimmy and his brother sold Sawkins and bought part of a coppice near the house called Wood Mead. Here each had a two-roomed shack and a plot of land surrounded by corrugated-iron fencing. Jimmy now saw no one except Tommy, who brought him provisions and looked after him generally.

He had always been something of a mystic—the diary is full of references to visions—and at Wood Mead he spent most of his time praying and reading the *Christian Herald*, copies of which were piled against the walls of the hut to keep out draughts.

In his new abode Jimmy slept in a large drawer raised a few inches off the ground. The only other pieces of furniture were a stool and a barrel which served as a table. His staple diet was a mixture of beans and brown sugar. This he cooked himself on a paraffin stove. Jimmy grew vegetables in his garden and kept bees and tame rabbits. To discourage visitors he rigged up a series of trip-wires, and he kept a shot-gun handy to deal with those who might evade the traps.

Over the years many newspaper-men tried to interview the hermit. Few succeeded. Fanny called on him in 1927, but he hardly spoke to her. He was no longer interested in the things of this world, and spent whole days in contemplation, a sacking shawl round his shoulders.

In 1940 Tommy was taken ill, and the vicar of Great Canfield, Mr Maryon Wilson, arranged for a Mrs Sales to look after both him and his brother. Jimmy grew very fond of this lady, and the two of them often prayed together and discussed religious matters. Once he said to her, 'If you ever see my door open and my boots lying outside, you'll know I'm dead.'

On January 18th, 1942, Mrs Sales remembered those words. The door of Jimmy's hut was ajar, a pair of boots lay on the step, and when she went through to the bedroom, she found that the hermit had died in his sleep.

Chapter Three

SMUGGLERS AND HIGHWAYMEN

From 1750 to 1840 Paglesham was the liveliest smugglers' haunt in Essex. For much of that time the leader of the Paglesham gang was William Blyth, known to his friends as 'Hard Apple'. He was born in the village in 1756 and lived there all his life. By day he acted as churchwarden and kept the village shop, and this double employment allowed him to show his supreme contempt for authority by using the pages of the parish books and records entrusted to his care as wrappings for bacon, butter and cheese.

On dark nights when the wind blew fair Blyth and his fellow smugglers would launch their cutter, the *Big Jane*, and make for Dunkirk, where Frenchmen awaited them. Casks of rum and brandy and bales of silk would be brought from hiding and quickly stowed aboard the cutter. Then her crew would weigh anchor and steal softly back across the Channel.

Once home the Paglesham gang hid their illicit cargo in the church tower or in the 'Owd Widders', three hollow elms that grew beside Pound Pond, near East Hall. There was sometimes as much as £200 worth of contraband concealed in the trees, while the smugglers waited for the right moment to deliver the goods to their customers.

Returning from France the *Big Jane* was often sighted by revenue men, who would immediately give chase in their cruisers. But Blyth outwitted them time and time again.

On one occasion the commander of a cruiser boarded the smugglers' boat and confiscated its cargo of brandy. While the kegs were being transferred from one boat to the other, 'Hard Apple' plied the officer and his crew with liquor until they became so drunk that they failed to notice that as fast as the brandy was lowered into the cruiser's hold the smugglers handed it back to the cutter. When the men parted, with much befuddled handshaking and cheering, Blyth had not only recovered his cargo but gained several casks that the excise cruiser had earlier taken from another smuggling vessel.

During another escapade William Blyth was caught by his arch-enemy, Mr Loten, the customs officer at Leigh, and after being bound hand and foot was thrust into the revenue cruiser's hold. Hanging was a common penalty for smuggling in those days and the outlook seemed black for 'Hard Apple' until his captor's boat ran aground on the Goodwin Sands.

Battered by the waves the ship was in imminent danger of breaking up, and the orders given by the captain only made things worse. Finally, at his wits' end, Mr Loten pocketed his pride and begged the smuggler to help him. Blyth laughed in his face. What did he care if the ship floated or sank, he asked, for if he escaped drowning he would most likely end up on the gallows. Seeing that there was no alternative, Mr Loten promised Blyth his freedom if he would shift the boat off the sands. To this bargain the smuggler readily agreed, and in a few minutes he had the boat out in deep water again. Loten kept faithfully to his word, putting Blyth ashore as soon as land was reached.

Exploits such as these earned 'Hard Apple' the grudging respect of the excisemen. He won the admiration of his cronies by deeds of bravado such as drinking whole kegs of brandy, crunching up and swallowing wine-glasses and, on one never-to-be-forgotten occasion, fighting the fierce Paglesham bull.

In their leisure hours Blyth and his gang of smugglers were fond of a game of cricket, and one afternoon they went to play in Church Field, where the bull was kept. Catching sight of the intruders the beast set up a terrific bellowing and charged, head down, tail purposefully twitching. Most of the smugglers jumped hastily back over the gate. But not William Blyth.

'Body and bones!' he yelled at the bull. 'Don't think to frighten me', and grasping a cudgel, he seized the animal by the tail and began to beat it about the ribs.

Startled by this treatment the bull turnèd and ran, blundering through hedges and into ditches in an attempt to escape its torment-or. But 'Hard Apple 'clung on to its tail and led the poor creature such a dance that it finally dropped down dead from exhaustion.

When in 1830 Blyth felt his own death approaching he asked his neighbour, Mr Page, to come to his bedside and read him a chapter from the Bible. After this had been done the old smuggler turned his face to the wall and murmured, 'Thank you. Now I'm ready for the launch.'

During the period of the Napoleonic Wars there was a merry band of smugglers at Great Bentley. They went in for rollicking midnight parties, at which they danced on empty spirit kegs and sang defiant ditties about excisemen. They hid their barrels of rum in a hollow willow-tree that grew in the gang leader's garden. Revenue officers frequently searched this man's house but discovered nothing. They never even bothered to glance at the innocent-looking willow by the cottage gate. The landlady of the 'Plough' at Great Bentley often received one of these barrels of rum. She was a woman of generous proportions, and once when word reached her that the excisemen were on their way to the inn, she ordered two confederates to go down to the cellar and fetch the illicit cask of rum, which she hurriedly concealed beneath her voluminous skirts. When the revenue men arrived they found a smiling landlady seated behind the bar, but not a drop of incriminating evidence.

A smuggler who lived at Great Stambridge in the early nineteenth century thought up an ingenious method of outwitting the authorities and silencing inquisitive locals. He spread rumours about a ghostly wagon that was supposed to haunt the country roads bordering the Crouch and Roach. And when the rest of the Stambridge smugglers landed illicit goods, he met them with a cart whose wheels, as well as the horses' hoofs, were muffled in thick white cloth. This vehicle, which the gang called the 'Ghost Bus', moved so noiselessly that it could pass through a village without anyone hearing it. Benighted travellers who saw the bus galloping along in the moonlight ran away in terror. This ruse worked well for many years, but in the end the customs officers caught most of the Stambridge gang and put them in prison. When they came to arrest the owner of the 'Ghost Bus', however, the excisemen found that he and his conveyance had disappeared. They were never seen in those parts again.

At Bradwell-on-Sea, in Georgian times, smugglers used the deserted chapel of St. Peter as a cache for liquor and lace. The chapel was believed to be haunted, and the men played up to the gullibility of the villagers and kept snoopers away by burning coloured lights inside the building. Hezekiah Staines, a famous Bradwell constable, would often work for the magistrates during the day and help the smugglers by night.

Throughout the years when smuggling was rife on the Essex Coast, highway robbery was prevalent inland, especially in Epping Forest. And it was here that in about 1690 a group of ruffians called the Waltham Blacks made their home. Most of them were ex-soldiers who had fought during the Civil War and, not being able to find employment afterwards, had turned highwaymen and deer-stealers.

By the 1720s the Blacks, under their leader, King Orronoko, had developed into a well-organised community. They looked upon themselves as a separate 'nation', and their kingdom now stretched from High Beech to Waltham Abbey. They had a strict code of conduct for their members, and any breach of the rules was severely and often bizarrely punished. On one occasion two offenders were blindfolded and buried up to their chins in earth. The rest of the Blacks then pranced round them, barking like dogs and snapping at their heads. Later the pair were allowed to go free.

When a man wished to join the fraternity he had first to prove that he did not babble in his cups by twice appearing drunk before King Orronoko. After that he had to provide himself with a fast horse, a brace of pistols and a gun for his saddle-bow. At the initiation ceremony the new member's face was smeared with soot—the distinguishing mark of the gang—and he was forced to swear on a stag's antlers never to betray the secrets of the group. He was then given a new name and was shown the list of Black tenets, the first of which read: 'There's no sin in deer-stealing'.

It was essential for a member of the Waltham Blacks to believe this, for hunting deer by moonlight was the gang's chief form of recreation. Cottages and inns on the outskirts of Epping Forest received the stolen venison, which went by the name of 'black mutton'.

Highway robbery was their main concern, however, and in the early eighteenth century hardly a day passed without a stage-coach or a private carriage having been stopped on one of the forest roads by a group of Blacks. These rogues also broke into country-houses on the edge of the forest, sometimes demanding money, sometimes just bottles of wine or brandy for their carousals.

In 1729 a Mr Woods became an unwilling guest at one of these feasts and afterwards wrote an account of his experience. He describes how he was travelling through the forest when his horse stumbled over a stone and lamed itself. He was thus compelled to spend the night at a small ale-house. Late in the evening a party of horsemen arrived at the inn, and when they entered the bar Mr Woods saw to his horror that their faces were blackened. He had discovered the rendezvous of the Waltham gang, and now, he felt sure, they would murder him.

But they did nothing of the sort. Very civilly their king asked him whether he would care to join them for dinner. Fearing to offend by a refusal Mr Woods accepted the invitation and was ushered into a room where, on a massive table, reposed 'eighteen dishes of venison in every shape: roasted, boiled with broth, baked collops, pasties, humble pies and a large haunch in the middle'. After bowing before King Orronoko the Blacks seated themselves round the table. A bottle of claret was placed at each man's elbow and the meal commenced. The robbers were in merry mood, laughing and singing and playing practical jokes. They treated Mr Woods as an honoured guest, and when the company broke up at 2 a.m. King Orronoko told him that they would be delighted to see him at supper any Thursday evening.

Mr Woods had no intention of taking the men up on their offer, but as he rode away from the inn later that morning, he could not help reflecting that the Waltham gang were not quite so black as their faces suggested.

A solitary highwayman who frequented the Epping district in the 1770s was John Rann, otherwise known as 'Sixteen-String Jack'. He was a flamboyant coxcomb whose clothes were always outlandishly original. He wore top-boots, ruffled shirts and natty crimson waistcoats. His favourite headgear was a hat covered with buttons and bound with silver strings. And his nickname came about because of the sixteen coloured ribbons that generally fluttered from the knees of his breeches.

One evening's 'work' on the Epping roads sometimes brought Rann as much as £100 in cash, as well as a valuable collection of rings, necklaces and watches. He was often caught, but lied with such cool impudence that he was acquitted six times before finally being found guilty.

In May, 1774, 'Sixteen-String Jack' appeared before Sir John Fielding, the Bow Street magistrate, accused of having stolen a gold watch from a Mr Devall. When asked whether he could offer anything in his defence the highwayman stared Sir John in the face and said, "I know no more of the matter than you, nor half so much neither.' On this occasion Rann wore 'a bundle of flowers in the breast of his coat, almost as big as a broom'. His leg-irons were decorated with bright blue bows. After hours of fruitless questioning he was set free.

Later in the same year Rann stole one watch too many. His victim this time was Dr Bell, chaplain to Princess Amelia, and there was no disputing his evidence. The highwayman was tried at the

Old Bailey in October and was condemned to death. The Sunday after the trial he had seven pretty girls to dine with him in his prison cell at Newgate. They laughed and joked far into the night, and 'Sixteen-String Jack' laughed loudest of all. He went to his execution at Tyburn on November 30th, 1774, in the same gay mood and showed not a trace of fear, for, as he said, the gallows was an object that he had 'long expected to see'.

Hanged at Tyburn in December, 1707, was Stephen Bunce, the most imaginative and amusing of all Essex highwaymen. His exploits read like tales by Hans Andersen, but they were real enough and finally brought him to the noose.

One day he was walking along the road to Romford when he saw a gentleman riding towards him on a splendid horse. Immediately Bunce threw himself down in the middle of the road and pressed his ear to the ground.

'What are you lying there like that for?' asked the gentleman, coming up to him.

'Ssh!' whispered Bunce, putting his finger to his lips.

'But what on earth are you listening to?' said the gentleman.

'Oh' replied Stephen Bunce, 'I never expected to hear fairies. This is the most lovely music I have ever heard, and I don't expect to hear such music again.'

Eager to share in this unique experience the gentleman dismounted and gave Bunce the horse's reins to hold. As soon as the gentleman was lying flat on the ground Bunce leapt into the saddle and galloped off to Romford. The horse went straight to an inn that was often used by its master and was recognised by the publican, who called out, 'Why, there's Mr Bartlett's horse!'

Keeping his wits about him Bunce told the landlord that Mr Bartlett was gambling at Ingatestone and was in need of fifteen guineas, for which he had been directed to leave the horse as a pledge. The money was forthcoming and Bunce went speedily on his way, well pleased with his booty.

On another occasion this cunning trickster was walking up a hill near Romford with a friend when ahead of them they spied an old farmer leading a donkey. Creeping softly up to the animal, Bunce slipped the bridle off its head and put it over his own head. His accomplice stole away with the donkey. At the top of the hill the farmer turned to mount his beast—and found himself confronted by a human being.

'I was not really a donkey but a man', Bunce hastened to explain. 'I committed a grievous sin and was transformed into a don-

2. "16-String Jack" enjoying a last drink in the condemned cell at Newgate.

key. But now I have atoned for my sin and have been changed back into a man.'

Gaping with astonishment the farmer released Bunce and went to the local market to buy another donkey. His own beast had by this time been disposed of and was up for resale. When he spotted the creature the old man shook his head sadly. 'What?' he said, 'Committed another sin already? I shan't buy you again.'

Chapter Four

PARSONS EXTRAORDINARY

Almost every evening throughout the early 1800s, a man wearing a bright yellow scarf, a pepper-and-salt coat and black pantaloons might have been seen walking from Maldon to Heybridge with a tea-pot clutched tightly in his hands. He was parson Francis Waring, returning home to Heybridge vicarage after collecting the tea-potful of beer that he always drank with his supper from the old 'Ship' inn at Maldon.

This singular cleric lived in a house as unusual as himself. The front door was a mock-medieval fabrication built of oak and plentifully studded with spikes and nails. A passage so narrow that stout Mr Waring had to sidle along it crabwise gave access to the downstairs rooms. This narrowness was the result of the parson's determination to construct a passage right through the middle of the house, and as the fireplaces and chimneys were already in the centre, the corridor had to be squeezed in between them.

The rooms at the vicarage were all papered with a light brown paper and furnished with logs of wood instead of chairs. Francis Waring slept with his wife in a huge wicker cradle on rockers. Although not poor, the couple ate off plain earthenware dishes and made their children feed from a wooden trough. There were no bells in the house, so the vicar summoned his family and domestics by whistling. He had a different warble for each person.

Every Wednesday Mrs Waring had to put on Quaker costume, as her husband was partial to this style of dress. He sometimes wore a Quaker coat. The vicar had a great variety of coats for morning, afternoon and evening wear, but his favourite was a leather one which had been made from a hide that he had himself taken to be cured in Chelmsford. Francis Waring was fond of weird headgear and frequently went to church in an old straw hat full of holes. More sinister was the black scarf that he occasionally wore during the service. Once when he went to visit a parishioner,

27

he found her engaged in making a bonnet for her daughter and was so struck by it that he asked her to make one of the same type for himself. A few days later he came to collect the bonnet, and clapping it on his head, tied the ribbons under his chin. Thus attired he drove back home to Heybridge.

Parson Waring's eccentricities of dress amused the inhabitants of Heybridge and Maldon, but they did not amuse the local bishop. On one occasion Waring attended a clerical function, wearing scarlet breeches and white stockings. The bishop was scandalised and called the parson over. Before he could remonstrate with him, however, Waring gave the bishop a dazzling smile and said, 'My Lord, that you should condescend to notice my breeches is an honour I did not expect—here is my tailor's card.'

Mr Waring's ready wit made him popular at dinner-parties in the neighbourhood, for he could be relied upon to make the evening hilarious with his jokes. Once at a civic dinner, Mr Bugg, the portly, pompous Mayor of Maldon, who looked very like a large bulldog, addressed Waring in an offensive tone. Whereupon the vicar looked him full in the face and gave a loud 'Bow, wow, wow, wow, wow.' Everyone burst out laughing and the mayor was effectively silenced.

In the pulpit, too, Parson Waring was brilliantly witty, and when he first came to Heybridge in 1798, people flocked to hear his sermons. But he was so irreverent that he soon lost support. The vicar had to take the services in Mundon church and St. Mary's, Maldon, as well as Heybridge on Sundays, so he was naturally pressed for time, but he raced through the prayers at such breakneck speed that the bewildered congregations could not make the responses. As the years went by his sermons grew shorter and shorter until they were hardly there at all, and before he began to preach he took a small travelling clock out of his pocket and placed it on the ledge in front of him. He thought that singing in church was a complete waste of time and always tried to pronounce the benediction before the choir could begin the last hymn.

On one occasion Mr Waring's parishioners at St. Mary's asked the Reverend Charles Matthew, vicar of All Saints, Maldon, to speak to their parson about his behaviour in church. Mr Matthew was a somewhat fatuous man, and after he had reprimanded Waring, the latter said simply, 'Charlie—when Balaam could not speak his ass spoke.' To tease him, Waring once put a notice outside All Saints, which read: 'The Gospel according to Matthew.'

When Francis Waring died in 1833, he was greatly missed, for whatever his shortcomings, he had been an original and amusing character, and it was felt that life in the Heybridge district would not be quite the same without his jokes and eccentricities.

A contemporary of Waring was Thomas Archer, who was born in London in 1750. He was educated at Eton and Cambridge and took orders in 1775. At Finchley, his first curacy, he married, but the young lady contracted a fatal illness soon afterwards and died at North Benfleet, where Archer next became curate. Instead of asking a fellow clergyman to officiate at his wife's funeral, as was customary, Thomas drove her remains to church himself and then coolly proceeded with the service. A few months later he married Susannah Page, the daughter of a Nevendon farmer.

In addition to North Benfleet, Mr Archer held two other curacies at that time, Rawreth and Canvey Island, and he spent his Sunday mornings galloping madly from church to church, conducting a hasty service in each. He became expert at reciting the benediction whilst hurrying down the aisle, and before his parishioners were off their knees he had leapt into the saddle and was riding hell-for-leather towards his next congregation.

After several years at Benfleet, Archer was made curate of first Danbury and then Prittlewell. Whilst in this latter village, he developed the smoking habit and every Sunday he walked to church puffing at his long clay pipe. When he reached the church he would tap out the ashes against the wall, refill the pipe and place it in a niche by the vestry door, ready for when he came out.

Thomas Archer was next appointed vicar of Southchurch, and when Princess Caroline, wife of the Prince Regent, stayed at The Lawns, a nearby country house, she would come to hear him preach. He was an imaginative orator and his sermons were both pithy and amusing.

The same cannot be said of the poems he wrote under the pseudonym 'Calliope'. Most of them are moralistic verses with dreary titles such as *The Triumph of Loyalty* or *Age and Honour*. A somewhat better poem, *A Practical Description of New Southend*, which was published in 1794, enjoyed a small measure of success, as did his *Victory of Copenhagen*, which appeared in 1801. But the rest of his poetry quickly sank into oblivion.

In 1815 Archer left Southchurch and was sent to Foulness Island. He remained in this parish until his death.

Always a keen huntsman, at Foulness Parson Archer was able to indulge his passion to the full. If he had any services to perform on weekdays which coincided with the hunt, he would wear his scarlet jacket under his surplice, and as soon as the ceremony was over would untie his hunter from the churchyard gate and join in the chase. Once when he was conducting a marriage service, a fox passed the open door of the church with the hounds close behind it, and he broke off in mid-sentence to shout, 'Tally-ho! Tally-ho!'

Archer rather prided himself on his huntsmanship and would deliberately choose the most difficult cross-country routes so as to show off his skill. But pride often comes before a fall, and in attempting to leap his horse over impossible barriers he sustained many serious injuries. On one occasion, when the parson had broken his leg, a neighbouring clergyman came to Foulness to take over his duties and found him in the vicarage kitchen, clad in a fancy dressing-grown and a tasselled nightcap, his injured leg resting on the kneading-trough.

Thomas Archer never did dress in a conventional way. For instead of the sober black worn by his brother rectors, his usual outfit consisted of a blue frock-coat, white corduroy breeches and grey worsted stockings without gaiters.

The vicarage at Foulness was a rambling old house and, like the Heybridge vicarage, it had no bells. So when Archer wanted his wife to come to his study, he would beat the handle of the hearth-brush loudly against the wainscot and call, 'Pug!' Pug was Susannah's nickname, but visitors not in the know were quite startled by this performance, not being sure whether a human being or an animal would answer the summons.

When Parson Archer grew too old to go hunting he took to reading novels. Unfortunately, for the last few years of his life he was almost totally blind, and in trying to make out the print he held the books too near the candle flame, with the result that the edges became charred. The other subscribers to the lending library were not pleased at finding burnt books on the shelves, and in the end the librarian was forced to make Archer pay full price for every book he damaged, so that it could be replaced.

Thomas Archer died on February 17th, 1832, at the age of eighty-two, and people came to his funeral from miles around. His eccentricities had captured the imagination of his parishioners, and tale of 'th' owd parson's doin's' were long narrated in the Rochford Hundred.

After these two giants, let us have an interlude of minor characters; clerical buffoons who step briefly into the limelight and then make their bow. First comes James Salt, vicar of Barling from 1793 to 1824. He was a zealous farming rector who turned his drawing-room into a granary. One night he took it into his head to sow mustard-seed by lantern-light, and placing numerous lamps in the field opposite his house, he set to work. Within minutes crowds of villagers appeared on the scene to help put out what they thought was a fire. The vicar was furious at this interference, cursed the men for blockheads and sent them back to bed. Mr Salt subsisted on a diet largely composed of dandelion leaves and peppermint tea. He lived to a ripe old age.

A more dangerous cleric was Thomas Heard, vicar of Takeley in the early part of the seventeenth century. After imbibing stronger potions than peppermint tea he became so drunk that he 'tumbled into ditches'. In one of his fits of drunkenness he ordered a fire to be prepared so that he could burn his wife and children. They were saved from this fate by the timely arrival of visitors.

Almost as dangerous was the Reverend John Crosse, a former Gosfield parson. When clergymen visiting his church preached sermons of which he disapproved, he was in the habit of suddenly pulling open the pulpit door, whereupon the hapless rectors risked falling out head first.

In the past, vicars often aired their grievances in the pulpit or chatted with members of the congregation during the service. A nineteenth-century vicar of Rochford once interrupted his sermon to call to the clerk, 'Is my son Jack in church?'

'No', came the reply.

A few minutes later the question was repeated and the same answer given.

'Confound it!' burst out the minister. 'I shan't have a cherry left on my tree by the time I get home.'

Ambrose Westrop, vicar of Great Totham at the beginning of the seventeenth century, was a brutal lout of a man, so often scorned by women that he grew to loathe them with a deadly hatred. His sermons were nothing but tirades against the female sex, in the course of which he told many lewd jokes. Sometimes he would address women who had offended him by name and scream abuse at them from the pulpit. At the end of one sermon he publicly took his brother-in-law to task for not paying his tithes. And on another occasion, after he had quarrelled with a man called Kent, he rounded off his discourse by saying, 'They tell me the Devil is in Harwich, but I am sure he is in Kent.'

When Ambrose was rejected by Ellen Pratt, a wealthy widow, he wrote 'Bonny Nell, I love thee well' on a piece of paper and pinned it to his cloak to annoy her. Another woman who rejected him was punished in an even more whimsical fashion. The parson went to visit her and when she opened the door, suddenly snatched up her 'head-geere' and rode off with it tied to his horse's tail.

But enough of this tomfoolery. In the wings two more famous Essex parsons—Henry Bate and Edmund Hickeringill—clamour for attention. Mr Bate, whom his biographer, Henry Angelo, calls 'as magnificent a piece of humanity, perhaps, as ever walked arm in arm with a fashionable beauty', was a gay gallant whose love of women involved him in a succession of duels and fist-fights that culminated in the notorious 'Vauxhall Affair'.

One evening in the summer of 1773, the newly ordained Bate was walking in Vauxhall Gardens with an actress named Mrs Hartley when a crowd of swells, including Fighting Fitzgerald, wicked Lord Lyttelton and Captain O'Bourne, stared at the lady so offensively that she burst into tears. Mr Bate sprang to her defence, a quarrel broke out and a meeting was arranged at the Turk's Head Coffee House in the Strand. The dandies came to the rendezvous accompanied by a Captain Miles, who turned out to be no military gentleman, but a prize-fighter. He had been instructed to insult Parson Bate, provoke him to attack and then give him a sound drubbing. But in the event the prize-fighter received such a licking from Bate that he had to be taken away in a hackney-coach.

Mr Bate was at that time editor of the *Morning Post*, which he had founded in 1772, and he published a lengthy account of the Vauxhall business. Thereafter the public looked upon him as a hero and he became generally known as the 'Fighting Parson'. Bate was a great believer not only in self-advertisement but in organising publicity stunts to promote the sales of his newspaper. On one occasion he hired a hundred men dressed in blue breeches and coats, yellow stockings and peaked caps to march round and round Piccadilly Circus, blowing trumpets, banging drums and waving flags with the name of the paper written on them.

In 1775 Henry Bate's father, the vicar of North Fambridge, died and he succeeded to the living. He remained in London, however, and appointed a curate to take charge of the parish. The Bates originally came from Fenny Compton, Warwickshire, where Henry was born in 1745. In former times the family had been immensely rich, but by the 1770s most of the wealth had been squandered, and to help support his eleven brothers and sisters Parson Bate began writing plays.

The first of these, *The Blackamoor Washed White*, was put on at

Drury Lane in February, 1776. But it only ran for four nights, as Fitzgerald and his confrères decided to have their revenge on the parson, and by overturning benches, extinguishing lights, hurling missiles at the actors and causing general pandemonium, achieved their purpose very well.

In 1780 Bate married Mary White, Mrs Hartley's sister. Shortly after the marriage he quarrelled with his fellow directors on the *Morning Post*, left that paper and started the *Morning Herald*.

The following year found him and his wife occupying rooms in the King's Bench Prison as a result of a libel on the Duke of Richmond that had earlier appeared in the *Morning Post*. They were there for twelve months. During this period Henry Angelo visited Bate frequently, and on one of these occasions the parson tricked his friend into spending a night in the prison. Angelo was very fond of cribbage, and Mr Bate got him so engrossed in his game that he forgot the time. When he wanted to leave he found the prison gates locked until morning. Although he was given a comfortable bed, poor Angelo did not sleep a wink. The atmosphere of the prison was too hateful to him.

Parson Bate left London in 1782 and bought the advowson of Bradwell-on-Sea for £1,500. When he first came to the village it was a desolate, dirty, plague-ridden spot with inadequate drainage and no roads. The absentee rector had allowed both church and rectory to crumble into ruins. Mr Bate changed all that. Over the next fifteen years he spent £30,000 of his own money building roads, improving drainage and repairing the church, the rectory and many of the cottages. He lived at the rectory himself and acted as curate.

In 1784 Mr Bate inherited a fortune from a relative and, in compliance with the will, assumed the additional name of Dudley.

Many of the parson's London friends came to visit him at Bradwell and were lavishly entertained. Bate-Dudley specialised in giving suppers at which all the dishes were from one particular foreign country; Spain, perhaps, Italy or France. And sometimes the guests would be asked to wear appropriate national costume.

Mr Bate-Dudley kept a pack of foxhounds at Bradwell and hunted regularly. On one memorable occasion a terrified fox scrambled up the ivy-covered walls of Creeksea church, hotly pursued by Parson Bate-Dudley and three pairs of hounds. The kill was made on the leads of the chancel.

Henry Angelo once boasted to the parson about his huntsmanship. He soon wished he hadn't, for the next time they went out his friend mounted him on a wild scamp of a horse that obeyed no commands, but simply tore along, bucking and rearing and leaping every hedge and ditch in sight. Riding an equally mettlesome horse dare-devil Dudley followed behind, cracking his whip and urging on the chase with shouts of, 'Go it, Nimrod! Pelt away, Harry, my boy!' At the end of the run Angelo was scratched, bruised and trembling in every limb, but he had managed to keep his seat.

Mr Bate-Dudley relished all kinds of danger and one summer he persuaded Angelo to sail with him from Harwich to Ipswich in a hurricane. Their boat was twice on the verge of sinking, much of the equipment was lost and they were constantly being drenched by spray, but when they landed at Ipswich the parson told Angelo that he had rarely enjoyed himself more.

In 1797 the incumbent of Bradwell died and Bate-Dudley presented himself to the living. The Bishop of London refused to institute him, however, believing that he was guilty of simony. The matter was taken to court, but by the time a compromise had been reached it was discovered that the right of presentation had passed to the Crown and that Mr Gamble, Chaplain-General of the Army, had been appointed. It seemed very hard that Bate-Dudley should receive nothing after all he had done for Bradwell, and many influential people pleaded with the Government on his behalf. Nothing came of their intercession, and the parson obtained no pecuniary compensation. He was given Church preferment in Ireland, however, where he lived from 1804 to 1812. In 1813 he was created a baronet and in 1817 he became a canon of Ely Cathedral. Sir Henry never forgot the unfairness of his treatment over the Bradwell living and died in 1824, still fighting to regain the benefice.

Edmund Hickeringill was born at Aberford, Yorkshire, in 1631. On leaving school he went to St John's College, Cambridge, and was later made a junior fellow of Caius. Already as a student he showed himself to be a man of fire and brimstone, burning with anger at the injustice and hypocrisy of the world. He spoke out against all forms of oppression practised by governments and religions, but his ridicule was so vitriolic that he aroused only hatred and contempt.

When Mr Hickeringill left Cambridge he embarked on a quest for truth that led him to sample one religion after another until he finally returned to his starting-point—the Church of England. In 1652 he became a member of Thomas Tillam's Baptist Church in Hexham, Northumberland. Within four months he had been ordained a minister of that Church and was sent to a parish in Scotland. Later in the year he became a chaplain in Cromwell's

Army. He soon found the discipline of both Church and Army intolerable, however, and in 1653 he resigned his chaplaincy, left the Baptists and joined the Quakers. Hickeringill remained with this new sect for exactly two months. By 1654 he had decided to be a deist, and he alternated between deism and atheism until 1662 when he suddenly applied to the Bishop of Lincoln to be ordained into the Anglican Church.

In October, 1662, Mr Hickeringill was appointed vicar of All Saints, Colchester. Apart from one short interval he kept the living until his death in 1708. Throughout the 1660s the Church in Essex seethed with dissent, and in this atmosphere Parson Hickeringill's anger grew ever more impassioned. His sermons against 'Popelings' and 'foule Dissenters' were terrible to bear, so venomous was his abuse. Hickeringill had many of these sermons published, and also began to write controversial pamphlets with such titles as *The Black Nonconformist* and *The Ceremony-Monger*. In these works Mr Hickeringill attacks the Pope, the Church of Rome and all 'magpie-dressed priests'. He writes with humour and imagination, but the effect is marred by his uncontrollable rage and his complete inability to stick to the point.

Within his first few years at Colchester this fiery divine had begun the battle with Henry Compton, Bishop of London, which was to continue even after his death. The quarrel originated because the bishop gave to his favourites some tithes that by right belonged to the vicar of All Saints. Hickeringill was furious, but he cunningly bided his time until in May, 1680, a splendid opportunity for denouncing Compton came his way. He was invited to preach at the Guildhall before the Lord Mayor of London, and he devoted the entire sermon to ridiculing a certain bishop who neglected worthy parsons and encouraged Dissenters. He made it quite clear which bishop he was referring to.

Henry Compton could not stand for this. In March, 1681, he ordered Hickeringill to appear at Chelmsford Assizes on a charge of barratry. The trial began 'about two of the clock and continued until after candle-lighting' and was a farce from beginning to end. The junior counsel for the prosecution mumbled so badly that he could not be heard, no one seemed able to accuse Hickeringill of anything definite and the false witnesses brought in by Bishop Compton contradicted one another hopelessly. Mr Hickeringill denied all the charges, and the jury pronounced him innocent.

In June, 1681, Parson Hickeringill was summoned to Doctors' Commons for performing marriages without banns or licences. He entered the courtroom with his hat on his head, and the judge, Sir Robert Wiseman, asked him to remove it. Hickeringill refused. The hat was snatched off by an attendant. The parson grabbed it back again. And this little comedy went on until the judge gave in and allowed Hickeringill to retain his headgear. Mr Hickeringill then proceeded to answer in Greek all questions put to him. Sir Robert became infuriated and ruled that 'an appearance in Greek be registered as a non-appearance'. He suspended Hickeringill from his living for three years. But the parson rejoiced. He had succeeded in his object of making the authorities look foolish.

Now that he had no parish duties to perform Hickeringill could really get down to the business of plaguing the life out of Henry Compton. He was insolent to the bishop whenever they met, talked scandal about him to all and sundry and maligned him on paper. In August, 1681, he published a pamphlet entitled *News from Colchester*, in which he referred to Compton as a 'bold, daring and impudent man' and accused him of having a part in the Popish Plot believed to have been organised to dethrone the king and bring back Catholicism. As a result of this slander Hickeringill was had up before Sir Francis Pemberton at Chelmsford Assizes in March, 1682, and was fined £2,000. In 1684 he was excused payment and allowed to go back to All Saints, after first having been made to apologise publicly for his 'scandalous, malicious and erroneous' words about the bishop.

The last court case in which Mr. Hickeringill was involved occurred in 1706. The parson owned land in Wix, and to annoy the local authorities he tampered with the rate books there. He was found guilty of the forgery and fined £400. Hickeringill distinguished himself at the trial by leaping about the courtroom and cocking snooks at the judge.

After this show of defiance Mr Hickeringill's hatred and anger seem to have left him and he spent the last two years of his life peacefully composing a long and flattering epitaph for his tombstone. When the parson died, Bishop Compton made a special journey to view his grave in All Saints and took revenge on his old enemy by ordering the following words to be removed from the epitaph: 'eminent both in war and literature, having fought with honour on land and sea, and evinced the power of his mind in excellent writings on various subjects'.

Hickeringill was not really defeated, however, for his pamphlets, so abhorred by the bishop, could not be removed, and are still available now to all who care to read them.

Chapter Five

WRITERS AND POETS

Margaret Lucas, destined to become the most famous authoress of her day, was born at St. John's, Colchester, in about 1623. Her father, Sir Thomas Lucas, died when she was an infant, leaving her and her seven brothers and sisters to be brought up by their liberal-minded mother. This lady held the opinion, rare in the seventeenth century, that youngsters should enjoy themselves, and she allowed her children to do very much as they pleased.

What Margaret liked best was writing verse and philosophy, and by the time she was twelve she had filled scores of fat notebooks with her efforts. Industriously she scribbled her way through her teens, only stopping now and again to take a solitary walk in Colchester, or to sew up one of the bizarre velvet dresses she was so fond of designing for herself. She rarely joined in her brothers' and sisters' amusements: their feasting, dancing and theatre-going, for, as she tells us in her autobiography, she was 'more taken and delighted with thoughts than in conversation or society'.

In 1643, however, Margaret suddenly took it into her head that it would be good for her as a writer to learn something about Court life, and she applied for and obtained the post of maid of honour to Henrietta Maria, Charles I's queen, who was then at Oxford. Lady Lucas tried to dissuade her daughter from accepting the appointment, believing that she was totally unsuited for such a position and would be unhappy at Court. Margaret was determined to go, however, and that autumn departed for Oxford in high spirits. But her mother's fears proved justified, for no sooner had she reached the Court than a great bashfulness overwhelmed her and she dared 'neither look up, nor speak, nor be in any way sociable'. The courtiers jeered at her shyness, mocked the curious home-made gowns she affected and laughed her literary pretensions to scorn. Within a few days Margaret was bitterly repenting her decision to serve Queen Henrietta Maria, but her pride would not allow her to return home. She remained at Court for two years, eventually accompanying the exiled queen to Paris.

In April, 1645, William Cavendish, the Duke of Newcastle, arrived in Paris and immediately went to pay his respects to Henrietta Maria. At the outbreak of the Civil War the duke had been made Captain-General of the king's northern armies. He was a brave man but had somewhat old-fashioned ideas about generalship, and in July, 1644, Cromwell defeated him at Marston Moor. After the battle Newcastle was left with no ammunition and no money with which to raise more troops. He considered, therefore, that he could be of no further assistance to the king, and embarked for Hamburg, where he spent the winter. Despite his defeat he was regarded as a hero, and all the unmarried ladies at the English Court in Paris vied with one another to attract his attention, for he was a widower and at fifty-two was still extremely handsome.

To everyone's astonishment the only girl William took any interest in was Margaret Lucas. He admired her trim little figure, thought her cranky dresses wonderful and delighted in her conversation. As he too was a poet and philosopher the pair had plenty to talk about, and while discussing such obscure questions as what the moon is made of and whether snails have teeth, they fell in love. On Margaret's side, to be sure, the love was more idolatrous worship of a being she considered to be truly godlike, but it was no less welcome to the duke for that, and he decided to marry her. The wedding took place in Paris towards the end of 1645, and after the ceremony the couple went to Rotterdam for six months before finally settling in Antwerp, where they spent the rest of their time in exile.

As Newcastle's estates had been confiscated by the Parliamentarians he was penniless and had to live on credit throughout his years abroad. He entertained lavishly, however, and expended large sums on horses, which he prepared for *haute école*. Margaret meanwhile was pouring out an endless steam of poems, plays and philosophical fancies. She wrote in a terrible scrawl, paying no attention to spelling and never stopping to correct her work, for, as she said, 'There is more pleasure in making than in mending' She disliked walking anywhere when she was composing a difficult piece in case the movement jolted the thoughts out of her head, and she was often ill through lack of exercise.

Until 1650 the duchess was content to write merely for her own enjoyment and had no wish to publish her works, but from then onwards her one desire was to get into print. The reason was that she had come to doubt the feasibility of personal survival after death. Total oblivion was a concept that terrified her, but she hoped that through her books at least part of her would 'live by remembrance in after ages'.

Her first book, a collection of poems, was published in London in 1653. Most of the verses take the form of ridiculous but rather charming quasi-philosophical speculations about the workings of nature. The following poem, *Of Fishes*, is one of the best:

> Who knows; but Fishes which swim in the Sea,
> Can give a Reason, why so salt it be?
> And how it ebbs and flowes, perchance they can
> Give Reasons, for which never yet could Man.

At the Restoration in 1660 the Duke and Duchess of Newcastle were at last free to return to England, and they chose as their home the duke's most secluded residence, Welbeck Abbey in Nottinghamshire. Here they lived together in perfect happiness, both of them writing plays and philosophy and showering admiration on one another's works. Margaret had no children, but William had two sons by his first wife, and they and their families often stayed at Welbeck. Otherwise the duke and duchess saw few visitors. They were still very much in love and felt no need for other people. Their mutual affection was laughed at by their neighbours, as was Margaret's impracticality. Indeed, she was so clumsy that her housekeeper would not allow her to help cook, bake or preserve, for fear she should 'ruin all', and she was incapable of spinning. But she did understand sheep-farming and tended her own small flock as a relaxation from writing.

In 1662 the duchess launched upon the world fourteen weird and incomprehensible plays. The scenes are for the most part quite unconnected and the characters, with names like 'Sir Peacable Studious'. 'Monsieur Vain-Glorious' and 'Madame Caprisia', are mere embodiments of virtue or vice. Soliloquys abound, some of them over five pages long, and there is not a speck of wit to relieve the tedium of all this verbiage. None of the plays were ever performed, and Margaret realised that as a dramatist she had failed.

For the rest of her life she concentrated mainly on publishing her philosophical writings, and with these, surprisingly enough, she won great renown. Many learned men, including university professors, paid serious attention to the theories she put forward, such as that 'cancer is produced by too much salt', snow is nothing but 'curdled water' and 'all winds come from Lapland'.

In 1667 the duchess was invited to visit the Royal Society. She and her husband came to London in April that year and remained there throughout the summer. Margaret went several times to the society and was shown every respect by the members. But she was not much respected by anyone else in London, and within a few weeks had in fact become the laughing-stock of the capital. For she looked very peculiar in her 'antique dress' and velvet cap, with her hair all tumbled down about her ears, and her face, according to Pepys, covered with 'many black patches because of pimples'. Her mannerisms were equally strange. When greeting a friend she would bow low to the ground instead of curtsying. and would then begin to talk very fast, accompanying her words with nods, winks and wild gestures. The duchess had by now lost every trace of shyness and delighted in telling risqué stories and in using colourful oaths. As Evelyn recounts, she also shocked by her custom of chatting to gentlemen 'in her bed-chamber after dinner'.

Before Margaret left London she published the biography of her husband that she had been writing off-and-on for some years, and with this work she reached the pinnacle of her fame. Men of letters all paid tribute to her, even those who had mocked her previous books being forced to acknowledge that this time she had produced a masterpiece.

Back at Welbeck the duchess turned once more to philosophy, and now she found that inspiration often came to her in the middle of the night. William's secretary, John Rolleston, was therefore required to sleep in the room adjoining hers, and when a thought struck her she would call out, 'John, I conceive, I conceive!' Whereupon the poor man had to rise and commit her musings to paper. Margaret never left Welbeck again, but spent her last years in solitude with the duke. She died on December 15th, 1673, and the following January her body was taken to London and buried in Westminster Abbey.

Thomas Day, author of the children's book, *Sandford and Merton*, was born in London on June 22nd, 1748. His father, a customs official, died when he was a few months old, leaving him an estate at Bear Hill, near Wargrave, Berkshire, worth £1,200 a year. At the age of eight his mother sent him to Charterhouse, and in 1764 he went on to Corpus Christi College, Oxford. Here Thomas became an ardent disciple of Rousseau. He believed that a return to nature was essential for human happiness and showed his contempt for the artificialities of polite society by assuming boorish manners and blunt speech. He went about barefooted and ceased to comb his long black hair. After three years at Oxford he left the university without taking his degree, as he scorned all titles and distinctions. Day next decided to study law and registered as a pupil at the Middle Temple. He only studied in a desultory way, however, spending most of his time gadding about the Continent, and although he was called to the bar in 1775, he never practised.

Mr Day's chief concern throughout his youth was to find a wife with whom he could settle in rural retirement and carry out his plans for improving the conditions of agricultural labourers— a class of men he esteemed and greatly wished to help. He wanted a beautiful, intelligent spouse, a paragon at once soft-hearted and stoically brave. And he thought that he was more likely to procure his ideal if he moulded her character himself. So in 1769 he went to the orphanage at Shrewsbury with a lawyer friend of his, James Bicknell, and adopted a twelve-year-old blonde, whom he named Sabrina. In order to have a second string to his bow he visited a London foundling hospital a few weeks later and from there took a dark-eyed brunette called Lucretia.

Day then left for France with his two prospective brides and for eight months lived with them in a house at Avignon. During this period he instructed the girls in literature, science and moral philosophy and allowed them to speak to no one but himself and each other. Lucretia he found to be 'invincibly stupid', and when the party returned to England in 1770 he apprenticed her to a milliner in London. He entertained more sanguine hopes of Sabrina, who was quick-witted and anxious to please, and renting a cottage in Lichfield, Staffordshire, he continued her education for another two years. When he came to test her endurance, she too failed him, however. She winced when he poured melted sealing-wax over her arms and screamed when he fired pistols at her skirts. This lack of fortitude shocked Day, who at once abandoned all thoughts of making Sabrina his wife. She was sent to boarding school until she was seventeen, and eventually married Mr Bicknell.

Thomas Day spent most of 1773 travelling abroad, after which he set up house in London and began to write poetry. He also wrote pamphlets advocating the abolition of the slave-trade and demanding higher wages for farm-labourers. He was still searching for his ideal woman, and in 1777 finally found her in the person of Miss Esther Milnes, a fellow writer who understood his aims and fully sympathised with them.

The couple were married in August, 1778, and the following

spring bought a house and a few acres of farmland in the remote
Essex village of Stapleford Abbots. The soil round about was considered to be some of the worst in England, but Mr Day was sure
that deep ploughing would render it fertile. When he and his wife
took possession of their house it was little better than a ruin and
masons were engaged to rebuild one of the upstairs rooms, which
was to have a new window put in. The work was begun and all
went well until the masons came to ask Mr. Day where he would
like the window positioned. Day didn't know and he didn't care.
He was far too busy conversing with his wife and superintending
her studies to have time for such foolish trifles as windows. So
he told the astonished builders to complete all the walls of the
room, adding that he would have a hole cut out for the window
at some future date when he had leisure to attend to it. That
period of leisure never dawned. The chamber remained window-
less, and what should have been the master-bedroom became Mrs.
Day's dressing closet, where she was forced to burn candles even
in daylight.

The life of this lady was made difficult in many ways, for her
husband would not allow her to keep any servants at Stapleford
Abbots and forbade her to dance or sing. She was compelled to
give up her harpsichord, as Day thought it wrong to own such
an instrument 'when the poor want bread'. And she had to wear
rough, homespun dresses. Because she loved Thomas, however,
she gladly obeyed him in everything.

By his farm-hands Mr Day was regarded as the perfect master.
He increased their wages in winter so that they could buy nourish-
ing food, repaired their cottages and provided medicines for those
who were ill. They worked hard to please him, therefore, but with
all their efforts could not make the soil less clayey, and after three
disastrous years Day had to admit defeat. He sold his Essex farm
and bought a more promising one at Ottershaw, Surrey, where he
continued to practise philanthropy.

In 1783 Day started to write *Sandford and Merton*. He completed
it in the summer of 1789, and in September that year set out on
horseback to visit his mother, who lived at Bear Hill. He had not
had his mount broken in as he wished the animal to be natural
and unrestrained. And unrestrained it certainly was, for at Wargrave it decided that it had had enough of its rider and tossed
Mr Day head first onto the road. He died almost immediately and
was buried in the town.

Another farmer-cum-writer was Charles Clark, who was born

at Heybridge in 1806 and educated at Witham Place School. In about 1830 he became the tenant of Great Totham Hall and took up farming. But he was really more of a scholar than an agriculturist and spent his leisure hours reading, writing verse and endlessly pondering the Malthusian principle, of which he was a firm supporter. He loathed children and considered women to be nothing but a pack of scheming jades. Men he got on with well enough, but he preferred books to any human beings and filled his house with rare tomes and pamphlets.

Shortly after his move to Great Totham, Clark acquired a private printing press and began to issue reprints of many of the curious old tracts in his possession. He was particularly interested in reprinting the work of Essex writers, and one of the first things to come from the press was a limited edition of Thomas Tusser's *A Hundred Good Poyntes of Husbandrie*. There followed poems by Francis Quarles and Robert Winstanley and a long misogynistical poem, entitled *Pleasant Quippes for Upstart Newfangled Gentlewomen*, by Stephen Gosson, a sixteenth-century parson of Great Wigborough. Pamphlets dealing with the Chelmsford witch trial of 1645 and the Fairlop Fair were also issued, as well as several Essex love letters and prayers by Essex divines.

Charles Clark naturally printed his own poems at the press, too, and these were written under various pseudonyms such as 'Clement Clodpole', 'Doggerel Drydog', 'Malthus Merryfellow' and 'Professor Plypen'. The majority of his poems deal with local events, and despite the use of colourful Essex dialect words are somewhat tedious. But he could write clever satire, and his best pieces are probably those in the booklet entitled *Metrical Mirth about Marriageable Misses, or the Modern Mode in Matters Matrimonial*, which was published at Great Totham in 1848. In this collection Clark pokes fun at matchmaking mamas, and the following stanzas from the poem, *The Mother's Advice to her Daughter*, exemplify his neat satiric style:

> My girl, you must not fall in love
>   With virtue or with wit;
> Unless there's rank, or money too
>   To gild the pill a bit.
> Wit's but a frothy thing at best,
>   And virtue stale becomes;
> Stick to the *solid pudding*, Jane,
>   And marry for the *plums*!

Don't ever let me hear you say
    A word of 'mutual flame';
That's not the way to win the trick,
    In matrimony's game.
Besides, such flame, though hot at first,
    Soon dim and quench'd becomes;—
Stick to the *solid pudding*, Jane,
    And marry for the *plums*!

'Tis very well for vulgar folks,
    To talk of hearts and darts;
But girls like *you*, should be above
    Such sentimental parts.
A knock! It is that lord so rich—
    Though he has toothless gums;—
Stick to the *solid pudding*, Jane,
    And marry for the *plums*!

Just move that ringlet, love, and as
    You sit, take care to show
That pretty foot, blush—if you can—
    That's it! You're perfect so!
I'll leave you to receive the peer—
    Here old Lord Liquorish comes;—
Stick to the *solid pudding*, Jane,
    And marry for the *plums*!

Every time Clark published a new batch of verses he would distribute them amongst his friends and neighbours. Any poems that were left over he tied to small gas balloons and sent fluttering off on aerial voyages. They would be found and appreciated, he hoped, by men in distant parts of the country.

As well as verse Charles Clark wrote a constant stream of letters to newspapers such as the *Chelmsford Chronicle* and the *Family Herald*, recommending population control and pointing out the miseries of 'brat breeding'. Throughout the 1850s he was collecting miscellaneous writings against philoprogenitiveness, which he planned to incorporate into a book to be called *Mirth and Mocking on Sinner-Stocking*. But in fact he never got further than issuing three broadsides of such pieces gathered from authors like Plutarch, Kyd and Don Juan. The first broadside is interesting because its title consists of one long alliterative sentence containing seventy-five words that begin with the letter 'p'. No word is used twice.

In 1853 Clark gave up farming left Great Totham and moved into Butterfly Hall, Heybridge. In 1862 he gave up printing and writing and lived in complete retirement, with only his beloved books for company. These he continued to collect in ever increasing numbers, until they overflowed from their shelves and were ranged in huge toppling piles on tables, on chairs, on the floor. Books invaded the kitchen and the cellar; blocked the passages and the stairs and were stacked up against walls and windows, shutting out the light. In these dim and dusty, but to him perfectly congenial surroundings Charles Clark spent his final years. He died in March, 1880, and was buried in Heybridge churchyard.

Chapter Six

SOME INVENTORS

Aaron Hill, popularly known as 'Hilarious', was both a writer and an inventor. He wrote seventeen plays, collaborated with Handel over the opera. *Rinaldo*, and composed much mediocre verse. But although most of his friends were authors and he kept up a literary correspondence with Richardson until his death, Hill regarded writing as something faintly frivolous and only indulged in it as a relaxation from what he considered to be the true business of his life—improving the lot of humanity through his schemes and inventions.

Born in London on February 10th, 1685, Aaron was compelled to use his wits from an early age, for his father, a solicitor, died penniless when he was an infant, leaving him in the care of his mother and grandmother. At ten he was sent to Westminster School. Here he earned his own pocket-money by doing his fellow pupils' homework and entertaining them with tricks and experiments.

In 1700 Hill learnt that Lord Paget, the English ambassador in Turkey was distantly related to him and he went out to Constantinople, hoping that his lordship would find some position for him. The ambassador was so impressed by the boy's enterprising nature that he treated him as a son, procured a tutor for him and later sent him on a tour of the East. Aaron accompanied Lord Paget when he returned to England in 1703, and was on the point of being adopted by the nobleman when a jealous female intervened and brought about a coolness between the two men.

Thrown back on his own resources once more, Hill spent the next six years travelling on the Continent, acting for much of that time as tutor to Sir William Wentworth, a young Yorkshire baronet. He finally settled in England in 1709 and immediately published *Camillus*, a poem in praise of the Earl of Peterborough, who had played an important part in the war of the Spanish succession. Flattered by this attention the earl made Hill his private secretary and introduced him to society.

In 1710 Hill married a Miss Margaret Morris of Stratford, and with her he received a considerable fortune. He now had sufficient income to be able to give up his secretarial post and devote his time to plans and projects, and by 1713 he had obtained a patent for his discovery that 'oil sweet as that of almonds' could be extracted from beech-mast.

He invented a special 'grinding engine' to crush the beech-nuts and sent agents round the country with barrels of the oil for doctors, perfumers and clothiers to sample. He also wrote a tediously long-winded pamphlet eulogising beech-mast, and with each pamphlet went a tiny bag containing some mast, so that the reader could taste its excellence for himself. By 1714, Mr Hill had found that there was a market for his oil, and in the autumn he started with other subscribers the Beech-Oil Company. Most of the nuts were obtained from beech-trees in Epping Forest. There was no lack of nuts and the venture might well have succeeded, but in 1716 bitter squabbles broke out amongst the shareholders and the company was dissolved.

Aaron Hill next decided to become a coloniser. He bought a land grant which would enable him to found settlements in Florida and Georgia and proposed to send out five hundred well-equipped pioneers. To raise money for ships and provisions he wished to hold a national lottery, but the Government rejected this idea and he was forced to abandon the whole scheme. Soon afterwards Hill submitted to the Government his plan for closing the Dagenham Breach. This too was rejected.

Nothing daunted, in 1718 Mr Hill published an article describing his latest invention—a highly combustible fuel made from coal-dust and 'that black owsy mud which is common on both sides of the Thames'. One shovelful of coal-dust was to be added to three shovelfuls of mud, and the mixture was then to be shaped into balls 'about the size of large cannon bullets' and left to dry in the cellar. These balls apparently burnt with a 'striking liveliness', but somehow they never caught on. Hill believed that they would be cheaper than any other fuel in existence, but as his instructions for their manufacture included buying a large hand-mill, hiring lightermen to dredge up the mud, carriers to deliver it and servants to mix it with the milled coal, the process sounded extremely laborious and was quite beyond the pocket of the average householder.

Every summer Hill spent some months on his estate in the north of Scotland, and in 1728 he noticed how thickly wooded were the banks of the River Spey. All those trees standing about idle might usefully be turned into ships for the Navy, he thought, and entering into an agreement with the landowners to whom the trees belonged, he hired a group of workmen to carry out his scheme. All went well until the log rafts had to be floated down river to the saw-mill. The Scotsmen considered that it would be dangerous to ride on the rafts, as the current was swift and rocks abounded, and even though Hill went on the first raft and blew up most of the rocks with gunpowder, the men retained their fear. After two trips they deserted him and went back to their jobs in the lead mines. From the trees that had been felled only one ship was built. This totally disillusioned Hill, who left the Highlands never to return.

In 1731 Mrs Hill died and Aaron designed for her a strange memorial representing Time toiling up a black marble mountain and being waylaid halfway up by Death. Hill had now to make a home for his three daughters, Astraea, Urania and Minerva and his son, Julius Caesar, and they lived for some years in Petty France, Westminster. Then in 1738 Hill decided to retire to the country. So he bought Hyde House, just outside Plaistow, which was at that time a little Essex village.

Here Mr Hill embarked on his final venture, and planting a hundred thousand vines in the grounds, he devoted his energies to producing a burgundy as good as that of France. Unfortunately the climate about Plaistow proved to be 'moist and malignant' and the grapes never ripened. Hill insisted on making wine with the green grapes, however, and sent bottles of it to all his friends. No one had the heart to tell him that it was filthy stuff, and he died at Plaistow in 1750, happy in the belief that he had achieved his object. He was buried next to his wife in the Great Cloister at Westminster Abbey.

Whereas Aaron Hill's enterprises all ended in failure, the projects of Henry Winstanley were remarkably successful, for he was a businessman as well as a dreamer and knew how to conduct his affairs to best advantage.

Henry's father left his birthplace, Winstanley Hall, near Wigan, Lancashire, in about 1640 and settled in Saffron Walden. He held various positions under the third Earl of Suffolk and was bailiff at Audley End from 1652 to 1655. Henry, who was born at Walden in 1644, early showed promise of inventive genius. While he was still a boy he was commissioned to repair the clock of St. Mary's church, and he not only mended it but, to the great delight of the townsfolk, added a mechanism whereby the rising and setting of golden orbs (which represented sun and moon) were accompanied by melodies played upon bells. He received £108 for this contrivance.

In 1665 Henry acted as a porter on the Audley End estate, but in his spare time he was busy designing a pack of geographical playing cards. This wonderful pack contained the usual fifty-two cards, but the suits were Europe with a rose emblem instead of hearts, Asia with a sun instead of diamonds, Africa with a crescent moon representing spades and America with a star representing clubs. Each card bore a picture of some city or State and an account of its history. The cards were issued in 1666 and quickly became popular.

Charles II bought Audley End in 1669, and the following year he made Henry Winstanley 'clarke of ye works' at the new palace. The young man was now earning enough to be able to build himself a house, and he chose a site on the Cambridge road, opposite Littlebury church. When completed the house was an imposing and original edifice with a lantern and a weathercock on the roof, a clock over the front door and a miniature windmill in the yard, which pumped water to the kitchen. The interior was filled with all sorts of tricks and gadgets. These were called 'Winstanley's Wonders' and were shown to the public for '12d each and to liverymen 6d'.

In one room lay a slipper that caused a ghostly apparition to rise up through the floor if anyone kicked it. And in another room was a trap-door that pitched unsuspecting visitors down into the chamber below. No chair in the house could be safely sat upon. One suddenly shot out two arms and imprisoned its occupier, another changed shape when touched and, by means of springs and pulleys, a third conveyed startled guests out into the orchard, up a tree and over a moat. In a secluded corner of the grounds there was a tempting lovers' seat which deposited whoever sat on it in the middle of the nearby canal.

In about 1675 Winstanley married a Miss Elizabeth Taylor, and leaving her in charge of the house he went to London to open his Mathematical Water Theatre, which stood at the lower end of Piccadilly. Here Henry produced brilliant displays of conjuring, using fire and water as his mediums. He created tableaux with jets of coloured water and devised strange mechanical curiosities such as flying dragons which spewed out perfume, water and tongues of flame. Admission charges were: 'Boxes 2/6; pit 2/-; first gallery 1/6; upper gallery 6d.', and within a few years his shows had become the most popular entertainment in town.

As well as running the theatre, Mr Winstanley maintained his post as clerk of the works at Audley End. He kept this position until the end of James II's reign. To please that monarch he made a series of twenty-four engravings depicting the 'Plans, elevations and particular prospects of Audley End Pallace'. These were issued in 1688 and show how truly magnificent the building looked in its heyday.

By the 1690s Winstanley had amassed a considerable fortune from his various enterprises and with part of this money he bought five trading vessels. In August, 1695, one of the ships was wrecked on the Eddystone, that treacherous reef on which so many ships had foundered. In October a second vessel, the *Constant*, was also lost on the reef.

Mr Winstanley was furious. He went to Plymouth, called a meeting of the principal inhabitants of the town and asked them whether it wasn't about time a lighthouse was put on the Eddystone. They agreed that it was necessary to place some sort of beacon on the reef, but told him that they had never found anyone willing to undertake such an arduous task. The Eddystone was fourteen miles out from Plymouth, landing on the reef was well-nigh impossible and even if it could be built, what lighthouse would withstand continual buffeting by waves and gale-force winds? Suddenly Winstanley knew the answer. His lighthouse. No one thought that a beacon could be erected on such barren rocks, but he, the famous inventor, would prove that it could be done. He returned to Littlebury and drew up a plan for his pharos. In 1696 he submitted the design to Trinity House. It was accepted, and work on the Eddystone was begun that summer.

For three gruelling years Henry Winstanley and his gallant team of workmen struggled with the elements, with hunger and cold; frustration and despair. Once they were marooned on the reef for eleven days, and another time a French privateer partially destroyed their work and took Winstanley captive. But they overcame all obstacles, and on November 14th, 1698, Henry climbed to the top of his lighthouse and lit sixty tallow candles. The light was visible from Plymouth and when they saw it the townspeople went crazy with joy. Some ran up to Plymouth Hoe to get a better view; others put to sea in rowing boats. All were shouting and cheering and throwing hats in the air. Winstanley had done it. He'd set a beacon on the Eddystone rocks. Now their ships and their men would be safe.

In 1699 the finishing touches were given to the lighthouse. When completed it was 120 ft. high and 24 ft. in diameter. The lower half was made of blocks of stone strengthened by iron bands; the upper portion was of wood, and the whole presented an extremely whimsical appearance. Carved round the sides were mottoes such as PAX IN BELLO and GLORY BE TO GOD. An enormous flag flew from the look-out point and surmounting the lantern was a weathervane. There were galleries and balconies, twiddly bits of ironwork and four giant ornamental candlesticks. Jutting out both sides were numerous cranes and pulleys and 'a moving engine-trough to cast down stones to defend the landing-place in time of need'.

Many people who came to inspect the structure doubted its safety, but Winstanley had such confidence in it that he longed for a violent tempest that would prove the building's strength. In 1703 his wish was granted. On the night of November 26th he was in the lighthouse carrying out some repairs when the Great Storm hit southern England and swept him and the building clean away.

Thus Mr Winstanley's venture ended in disaster, but it facilitated the more successful enterprises of Smeaton and Douglass. And in recognition of his services to the nation his widow was granted a pension of £100 a year on condition that she did not remarry. Soon afterwards Elizabeth did in fact marry the French painter Tessier. As the couple kept on Winstanley's theatre and his house at Littlebury they were very well-off, but Elizabeth was so greedy for money that she concealed the match and continued to draw the pension until her death.

Throughout the latter half of the seventeenth century there lived 'up one pair of stairs, at the sign of the Anodyne Necklace, just by the Rose Tavern, without Temple-Bar' that arch imposter, Paul Chamberlen. Paul was the great-grandson of William Chamberlen, who invented the midwifery forceps, and his father, Peter Chamberlen, was a distinguished physician until his last years, when he became mad. In about 1649 Peter bought Woodham Mortimer Hall, near Maldon, and Paul, who was born in London in 1635, grew up there. He returned to the hall for frequent visits until his father's death in 1683.

After receiving a university education Paul successfully practised obstetrics, but he was best known as the inventor and tireless advertiser of the 'celebrated anodyne necklace', a string of small beads 'about the size of barleycorns' which was supposed to help babies' teeth come through. It also protected the infants from illness and death, 'producing all these surprising effects from a secret harmony between this necklace and the human body'. Women in labour who wore the necklace were assured of 'an extraordinary easy time . . . for from the insinuating figure of its alcalious atoms and effluvia it will act in regard to delivery as it does to let the teeth out of the locked-up gums of children'. A bottle of 'liquid coral' to rub onto babies' gums went with each necklace and the two together cost five shillings.

To boost his reputation Dr Chamberlen wrote under false names an endless stream of pamphlets and articles praising his quack remedies. Sometimes the pamphlets purported to come from the pen of an 'anonymous admirer', and once he even dedicated a book to himself and 'the learned members of the Royal Society'.

Dr William Swallow, a contemporary of Chamberlen, had a large practice in the Dunmow area. His patients included Lady Maynard, of Little Easton Lodge, and Robert Rich, second Earl of Warwick. Aided by a fertile imagination and a smattering of astrology he invented innumerable weird cures for the flux, fistula, consumption, 'hysterickes' and "fitts'.

'Snayle milk' was very good for consumption, he believed, and to cure a 'delirium in the heade' there was nothing quite like a dish of 'pickled herringe'. The doctor's favourite remedy for toothache was a mixture of peppercorns, rosemary, powdered oyster-shells, honey and vinegar 'applied in a fine ragge'. But medicine made from salt and ground-ivy would do as well—provided the ivy was picked 'at ye fulle moon'.

To the feet of patients who were subject to fits and 'talked idely' Dr Swallow tied a brace of dead pigeons. They apparently 'dide well' on this treatment. Many of his patients suffered from gout and his advice to these gentlemen was to 'take a rabbitt hott and slay ye skin off and applie it to ye gouty place as hott as it comes from ye flesh'. For inflammation of the ear he recommends applying 'rosted crabbs as hott as you can suffer them'.

Crabs loom large in many of the doctor's remedies and are included in the most fanciful of all his cures, which he laconically labelled 'A Powder'. His instructions for preparing this concoction are: 'Take of the blacke topps of crabbs' claws, of ye hores hound, of red coral, pearls, white amber and ye bone that is found in ye head of a hawke. Mash all up and make into balls. The crabbs must be gathered in June when ye sunn is in consor'.

Chapter Seven

SOME SPORTSMEN

At midday on August 1st, 1883, a huge candy-striped balloon named *The Colonel* rose from the paddock adjoining the Maldon gasworks and, to the accompaniment of hearty cheers, floated off over the River Blackwater. On board were Mr Joseph Simmons, the aeronaut, and that intrepid adventurer, Sir Claude Champion de Crespigny. They passed Osea Island and Bradwell at a height of 8,000 ft., and then slowly climbed to 17,000 ft.

When the balloonists descended through the clouds late in the afternoon, they saw beneath them the Dutch town of Flushing. Over rooftops they skimmed; over trees and fields. The grapnel was thrown overboard and caught in a ditch. Back jerked the balloon, and the car did a double somersault which very nearly upset its occupants. They managed to save themselves, however, by clinging firmly to the guy-ropes. After they had landed and packed up *The Colonel*, Sir Claude and Mr Simmons ate a celebration dinner at the Wellington Hotel, Flushing. They had just become the first men to cross the North Sea in a balloon. For his part in the achievement Sir Claude was later presented with the gold medal of the Balloon Society of Great Britain and the international medal of the Royal Aero Club.

This exploit typifies the sort of adventure the baronet most enjoyed. Always he loved to perform the dangerous, the exciting, the unusual feat, and he exalted in such deeds as ends in themselves. His was the spirit of the knights of old, who lived to prove their courage, and this is not surprising, for his ancestors belonged to the Norman family of the Marmions, that warlike clan described by Scott in his poem, *Marmion*. Sir Claude's father was descended from a branch of this family, the Sieurs de Crespigny, who settled in England after the revocation of the Edict of Nantes in 1685. His mother was the second daughter of Sir John Tyrrel, of Boreham House.

Sir Claude was born in London on April 20th, 1847, and at thirteen he entered the Navy. Five years later he transferred to the Army, joining the King's Royal Rifle Corps. The regiment was then stationed in Ireland, and here he took up steeplechasing. So recklessly did he gallop about at this time that he was known as 'The Mad Rider'. In India, to which his regiment was ordered in 1867, he continued steeplechasing and acquired a taste for big-game hunting.

On the death of his father in 1868, Sir Claude succeeded to the baronetcy. In 1870 he resigned from the Army and returned to England. He married a Miss Georgiana McKerrell in 1872, and after living in Wiltshire for some years, the couple moved into Champion Lodge, Great Totham.

Menservants who wished to work at the lodge had first to have a boxing match with Sir Claude. Only those who showed plenty of spunk were hired. The baronet employed this method of choosing his domestics until he was well into his sixties. He was extremely fond of boxing; so fond, indeed, that if he met a strong-looking tramp whilst out walking, he would challenge him to a fight in exchange for a meal. Knowing his weakness for a bout of fisticuffs his friends once engaged a professional pugilist, dressed him up in old clothes and made sure that he came to Sir Claude's notice. The baronet received a sound thrashing on this occasion, but he took it all in good part and continued to issue his challenges.

Sir Claude hunted regularly with the East Essex hounds, and when out with the pack one day in February, 1881, he performed an amazing act of bravado. The fox was found in a covert near Champion Lodge and made for Goldhanger Creek, where it crouched on a small island three hundred yards from shore. The hounds lost the scent, but Sir Claude was not going to let Reynard escape, and taking off his hat and coat he plunged into the icy water and swam to the island, followed by the dogs. The two leading hounds drowned the fox, and its body fell into the water, but Sir Claude dived down and retrieved it. By this time a boat had been sent to fetch him back, and he returned to his delighted fellow-huntsmen, proudly bearing his trophy aloft.

Later in 1881 the baronet laid out a steeplechase course in the fields around Champion Lodge, and annual race meetings were held there for many years.

In May, 1886, Sir Claude de Crespigny went to London to see Blondin tight-rope walking at the Albert Hall, and after the show he asked the acrobat if he would take him across the rope with him. Blondin refused. The baronet received a second refusal when in the autumn of that year he requested to be allowed to join Stanley's expedition in search of Livingstone. He was told that although physically fit he could not do so as he had insufficient knowledge of Central Africa. Bitterly disappointed, in December Sir Claude went off to America to shoot wild turkey. The trip was successful and he also shot a number of moccasin snakes.

When he returned to England the following summer, Sir Claude took up yachting and frequently went out on the Blackwater with his sons. He taught the boys to swim by simply pushing them overboard. In June, 1889, the baronet sailed round to the South Coast in a small open boat and then crossed the Channel in her. In July he booked a passage on a somewhat larger vessel and travelled out to Egypt, where he surprised the natives by swimming the Nile rapids.

The baronet spent the next few years hunting, shooting and steeplechasing in England. On January 21st, 1893, he was riding his favourite mount, Corrèze, at the Lingfield steeplechase when the animal fell and he was thrown off and kicked on the head by another horse. He sustained severe concussion and had to have stitches put in, but three days later, swathed in bandages, he was out rolling the cricket pitch at Champion Lodge. And on January 27th he was riding again, this time at Hurst Park. He did not give up steeplechasing until he was sixty-seven.

Early in 1905 Sir Claude de Crespigny and his son Vierville, went out to East Africa for some big-game hunting. They shot rhinoceros and hippopotamus and tried to add the 'jackets' of two man-eating lions to their collection of hunting trophies. The beasts eluded them, however. Whilst in Africa they ate hippopotamus-tail soup, ostrich-egg omelettes and baked eland.

After this expedition Sir Claude concentrated less on hunting than on other sports such as ballooning, 'aeroplaning', rowing, swimming and walking. In 1908 he walked from Champion Lodge to the Grand Hotel in London (a distance of forty-five miles) for a bet of 2/6. And in the last years of his life walking was his chief form of exercise. The baronet continued to go for long cross-country rambles right up to his death, which occurred on June 26th, 1935, when he was eighty-eight.

Dr John Salter, who lived at D'Arcy House, Tolleshunt D'Arcy, from 1864 to 1932, was a great friend of Sir Claude and a man of similar interests and outlook. The eldest son of a country gentleman, he was born at Fittleworth, Sussex, on July 14th, 1841. At the age of nineteen he enlisted in the Seventh West Herts Rifles as an ensign and within six months had been given command of his corps. In 1861 he became a student at King's College Hospital, London, where he spent the next three years.

John was a first-class pugilist and during one holiday he joined Hogini's circus as a prize-fighter, calling himself 'Jack O'Reilly'. On Derby Day in June, 1862, he engaged in a boxing match with a gipsy at Epsom Downs, which cost him his right eye. The retina was so badly damaged that he was unable to form proper images with it, and a few years later he had the eye removed and a glass one substituted. He never referred to this handicap and did not let it interfere with his life in any way.

In 1863, Dr Salter was offered the post of assistant house surgeon at King's College Hospital, but he preferred to work in a country district, and after beng made a member of the College of Surgeons in June, 1864, he bought the Tolleshunt D'Arcy practice from Dr Walker who was retiring. In September that year he took possession of D'Arcy House and in October he married his childhood sweetheart, Laura Duke.

When he returned from honeymoon, the young doctor quickly became a favourite in the village and surrounding area. He had a perfect bedside manner and took a genuine interest in his patients. Often he was out on his rounds in a pony-trap for eight or ten hours at a stretch. And he never minded being called in the middle of the night, but after dark the patient had to provide the doctor's transport, for he would not allow his pony to be overworked.

As well as carrying out his medical duties Dr Salter found time for a variety of sports and hobbies. He collected stamps, painted in oils and water colours and turned the meadow next to D'Arcy House into an exquisite flower garden. He attended horse shows, dog shows and race meetings.

From 1865 to 1929 he rented the Old Hall marshes near Tollesbury, and shot there whenever he could get away. Birds such as snipe, teal and wild duck were plentiful, and once he brought down so much game that the wagon carting it off snapped in two. He and his dog, Prince Rupert, had quite an adventure on the marshes one winter's morning in the 1880s. The animal swam out to fetch a teal that was lying on the ice some fifty yards from shore, but was so cold by the time it reached the bird that it fell down in a faint and was unable to get up. Dr Salter called the dog repeatedly, but when it still did not move, he got onto a floating ice raft and went off to the rescue. He just managed to revive the dog with brandy and bring it back to land before the raft disintegrated.

In 1898, Dr Salter went to Russia to judge sporting dogs in Moscow. He was at this time vice-president of the Kennel Club and a world-famous judge of dogs. Whilst in Russia he became friendly with the Czar and Grand Duke Nicholas, who took him bear-hunting. The doctor shot two brown bears, and had the beasts stuffed and shipped back to England. He kept them as ornaments in his drawing-room. On a second trip to Russia, in the winter of 1901, when Salter was the guest of Prince Youssoupoff at the Palais Rouge, he was invited to go wolf-shooting. He had not brought any shooting trousers with him, so decided to 'make shift with pyjamas'. The hesult of going out in the snow in such thin garments was, predictably enough, 'a nasty sore throat and a head cold'. Four stuffed wolves also resulted from the excursion, and these later joined the bears in the drawing-room.

Mrs. Salter became fatally ill in August, 1904, and heartbroken at the thought of losing her, the doctor made her promise that if she was able to she would return to him as a spirit after death. She died that September, but to her husband's sorrow never appeared to him. He felt unbearably lonely without Laura, but his pets were a consolation, and at night one of the dogs slept at the end of his bed, while a cat snuggled next to him on the pillow. At breakfast and supper this cat had its meals on the table-top.

Dr Salter's numerous activities also helped to lessen his grief, especially motoring. Early in 1902 he had bought the first car in D'Arcy, a Benz ideal, which he exchanged in 1904 for a Panhard, and in these vehicles he had some hair-raising experiences and not a few crashes. He always managed to escape serious injury, but after a collision with the Birch Rectory gate-posts he records that he had 'a large map of the world' on his thigh and buttock. The doctor was a keen gardener, and in the years before the First World War he won many prizes for his own blooms as well as judging roses for the Royal Horticultural Society. In 1909 he was elected a member of the Executive Council of the Essex Conservative Association, and he worked hard to further the aims of the party. He belonged to the British Legion and the Ancient Order of Foresters, and in his seventies became provincial grand master of the Freemasons.

When war was declared in 1914 Salter was made special constable for Tolleshunt D'Arcy, and he started a volunteer corps.

For the next few years he rarely got to bed before dawn, so busy was he searching for Zeppelins or operating on wounded soldiers. And yet, in the midst of war work, he found time to note in his diary that a pair of nightingales had nested in his garden and were singing beautifully.

On the doctor's eightieth birthdy in 1921, all the inhabitants of Tolleshunt D'Arcy assembled at the village school to wish him happiness and present him with a silver lamp as a token of their esteem. Salter lost none of his energy on becoming an octogenarian. He kept up his large practice, continued to attend society meetings and went out shooting in all weathers. At the age of eighty-seven he often worked in his garden for up to nine hours a day, and he was haymaking at eighty-eight.

Strenuous exercise kept him fit, Dr Salter believed, and certainly his health was remarkably good. He ate an onion every night to prevent liver troubles, and between breakfast and lunch took his 'remedy for old age'—a biscuit and a glass of white port. But pleasant as this cure undoubtedly was it could not ward off the effects of advanced age for ever, and in 1931 the doctor found that he frequently felt tired and had to rest. In March, 1932, he became ill and took to his bed. He died on the 17th April, aged ninety-one.

Another Essex sportsman who lived to be over ninety was Sir Thomas Barrett-Lennard, of Belhus, near Aveley. Born in December, 1826, son of Thomas Barrett-Lennard, M.P. for Maldon, and grandson of Sir Thomas Barrett-Lennard, the illegitimate son and heir of the Seventh Lord Dacre, he was educated at Harrow and Peterhouse, Cambridge. After spending some years on the Continent, in 1853 he married Emma, fourth daughter of Sir John Page-Wood, of Rivenhall Place. In 1857 he succeeded his grandfather at Belhus and settled down to the life of a country squire.

He went fishing, hunting and shooting, kept the South Essex foxhounds and had a first-class stud of pointers. But he was too tender-hearted to really enjoy blood sports, and later gave them up for steeplechasing.

Sir Thomas was passionately fond of his pet dogs of which he always had a large number, and when they died each one was placed in a coffin and accorded a solemn funeral. Dressed in a white robe, and accompanied by a footman bearing the coffin, the baronet would make his way to the canine cemetery that had been laid out in a corner of the Belhus grounds, and as the dog was lowered into its grave, he would read prayers from the

Anglican burial service. He would then return to the house, confident that everything possible had been done for the animal's soul.

Barrett-Lennard loved horses even more than he loved dogs. He trained ponies to sell at the annual Belhus horse fair that he started in 1875 and judged hunters at Essex shows. He could instantly soothe frightened or fidgety horses, and the most intractable mounts became mild as milk when he rode them.

As he grew older Sir Thomas lost all interest in his appearance and went about in very shabby clothes. Rather than put his butler to the trouble he would always open his own front door and was frequently mistaken for an under-servant. On one occasion he opened his park gates to allow a carriage to pass through and was given a shilling tip.

In about 1900 he became chairman of the Essex Asylums Committee, and when the committee met at Brentwood mental hospital he was in the habit of walking there and back across country—in a dead straight line. This meant that he had to jump ditches, climb fences and crawl through hedges. And on one return trip Sir Thomas was scrambling out of a hedge when he came face to face with a policeman. The bobby had been observing his antics for some time and now asked him where he thought he was going.

'To Belhus', answered his lordship.

'And where have you come from?' persisted the sergeant.

'Brentwood lunatic asylum.'

'Aha! I knew it', cried the bobby, and seizing a bewildered Barrett-Lennard by the scruff of the neck, he marched him back to the hospital. It was only with the greatest difficulty that the staff managed to persuade him that Sir Thomas was not a patient but a member of the committee.

At Cambridge the baronet had been a fine classical scholar, and when he was no longer able to follow outdoor pursuits, he turned to sporting with words. His last days were spent writing riddles in Latin and translating nonsense poems into Greek.

Sport of a very different kind was once enjoyed by Mr Nehemiah Perry, a farmer who lived at Strethall Hall, near Littlebury. In his youth this gentleman had married a gorgeous gipsy wife, but he soon tired of her and kept her hidden away on a farm he owned at Catmire End. The gipsies never forgave him for his callous treatment of the girl, and one night in March, 1849, they took their revenge by breaking into his house and attempting to steal his jewels and plate. As Strethall Hall was in rather an isolated position Nehemiah always slept with a loaded fowling-piece by his bed, and when he heard the marauders he rushed out and shot their leader dead. Realising that he meant business, the rest of the gang quickly made themselves scarce.

At the inquest the coroner highly commended this method of dealing with scoundrels. The dead man was identified as Little Abel, a well-known thief, and Perry talked of nailing the corpse to his barn door as a deterrent to future burglars. In the end he adopted a more lucrative scheme, and placing the body in Strethall church, he allowed visitors to view it at a charge of threepence each.

Nehemiah often sent hampers of game to his physician, Sir George Paget, and when the corpse became too offensive to exhibit he bundled it into a basket and dispatched it to the doctor at Cambridge, accompanied by a note that stated simply, 'This time I have shot a man.' Sir George was horrified to receive such a grisly present and at once handed it over to the Cambridge Anatomical School, which kept the skeleton for many years.

In 1842 there resided at Burton's Farm, Barling, an eccentric tenant-farmer whose idea of a pleasant afternoon's sport was to round up the women who had come to glean on his land. Attaching a rope to the heads of their horses he and his servant galloped along, tripping up maidens right left and centre and finally encircling them in the middle of a field. For this irresponsible behaviour the farmer was later summonsed and heavily fined.

One autumn day in 1914 a man suspected of being a German spy was brought before the magistrates at Woodford. Policemen had found him sitting up a tree in Epping Forest, dressed in ragged shorts, climbing boots and an alpine hat, and although he explained that he was only a camper, he had been hauled down from his perch and arrested. Learning of his predicament, the man's friends arranged for reliable witnesses to attend the hearing, and these gentlemen were able to convince the magistrates that their so-called German spy was none other than Millican Dalton, the famous mountaineer, president of the British Association of Cycle Campers and the Camping Club.

Mr Dalton was released, and immediately went back to his camp-site in the forest. He had always loved the outdoor life. During his boyhood in Cumberland he spent every available moment walking, cycling and camping, and when his family moved to Hale End, near Woodford, in the 1880s, he continued these activities in Epping Forest. As a young man he worked for a time in an insurance office in London, but he soon realised that the job did not suit him, and with his brother, Henry, he started a firm of tent-makers. He also acted as a guide on camping tours in Switzerland, Scotland and the Lake District and became renowned for his skill as a climber.

At Hale End Mr Dalton was known to the children as the 'Professor of Adventure', for he taught them how to make rope-ladders, build tree-houses and go tracking like Red Indians. He invited them to share his delectable if rather cindery camp-fire suppers and would afterwards tell hair-raising ghost-stories. In winter he arranged skating parties on the ponds in Epping Forest, and one year he showed the boys how to fashion simple skates out of wood. Normally the professor was a strict non-smoker, but he liked to puff at a cigar whilst skating. He said it helped him keep his balance.

Millican Dalton's clothes were a source of amusement to children and adults alike. He made his own corduroy shorts and breeches but could not be bothered to hem them, so the ends were always frayed. In summer he wore loose, open-necked shirts and in cold weather a Scotch plaid.

Throughout the 1920s and 30s Mr Dalton lived in a cottage at Baldwin's Hill, Loughton, and continued to bivouac in the forest. But he later moved to a district in Buckinghamshire called High Heavens. He died there in 1947, at the age of eighty.

Chapter Eight

TWO CORPULENT GENTLEMEN

Thomas Wood, the celebrated Billericay miller, was born on November 30th, 1719. Both his parents had hearty appetites and were fond of the bottle and they early encouraged these habits in their son. As a result he grew up to be a stout and sickly child with a repertoire of ailments that included vertigo, rheumatism and indigestion. When he was thirteen Thomas had an attack of smallpox, and this disease scared off all his other symptoms, which did not reappear until he reached middle-age.

Meanwhile he paved the way to trouble by devouring huge helpings of fat meat, pudding and cheese and washing them down with quarts of ale. Vegetables he rarely touched and he disdained fruit altogether. By the time Wood was forty he weighed about twenty-five stone and was growing larger every month. The names 'Ghastly Miller' and 'Monster Miller' began to be applied to him, but this did not make him alter his diet. For he argued that he felt perfectly fit and saw no reason to eat less.

His state of well-being was too precarious to last, however, and at the age of forty-three he again suffered from headaches, backaches and stomach pains. He lost his voice and most of his teeth, developed a raging thirst and was tormented by gout. He had heartburn and epileptic fits. But worst of all was the terrible feeling of suffocation that came over him after meals.

Sunk in despair, Thomas Wood was near suicide when in August, 1764, his friend, the Reverend John Powley, lent him a copy of Luigi Cornaro's *Discourses on a Sober and Temperate Life*. Cornaro was an Italian nobleman who led a dissipated life until he was forty, when his self-indulgence gave rise to infirmities similar to those suffered by Wood. The doctors told him that the only cure was to go on a diet. He took their advice, found that sobriety could give both health and happiness and followed a strict regimen to the end of his days. He was over a hundred when he died at Padua in 1566.

Inspired by Luigi's glowing account of the temperate life, Thomas decided that he too would diet. During the winter of 1764 he cut down on meat and restricted himself to one pint of ale a day. By the following spring his health had greatly improved and, encouraged by this, he left off ale and drank only water. In 1766 he gave up liquids altogether and never drank anything but medicine again. Wood got the curious idea that liquids were bad for him because one lunch-time his servant forgot to bring him any water and after that meal he felt better than ever before.

In 1767 Thomas gave up meat and cheese, and for the next two years he subsisted entirely on his own brand of pudding. Before going to bed he poured three pints of skimmed milk over a pound of crushed sea-biscuit. In the morning two eggs were added to the mixture and the whole was boiled in a cloth for one hour. It was then firm enough to be cut into portions.

At about this time Thomas discovered that he could digest his food better in the early part of the day. So he rose at one o'clock in the morning and breakfasted at four; ate his 'supper' at noon and went to bed at seven or eight in the evening. On this regimen he flourished gloriously. His voice came back, his aches and pains vanished. He began digging in his garden again and going for rides. Lifting quarter-ton sacks of flour was nothing to him now, and he ran up and down the mill steps as nimbly as a child.

All this exercise might have been expected to give Thomas a thirst and make him perspire, but he found that with his changed eating habits he never felt thirsty and did not exude a single drop of sweat. Another interesting discovery was that he had ceased to feel the cold, and that although he wore thinner clothes than before, his usual bouts of winter catarrh did not recur.

Mr Wood was never actually weighed, as he believed that this would bring him bad luck, but his doctor calculated that during the first two years of his regimen he lost at least ten stone. Thomas was still not satisfied, however, and ruthlessly eliminating eggs from his diet, he concocted a new pudding made from a pound of coarse flour and one and a half pints of either skimmed milk or water. He lived on this glue-like substance for fifteen years. And when he attended Romford market he always took some flour in his pocket and at lunch-time asked one of the innkeepers to boil him up a pudding. His friends were dismayed to see him eating such horrid food, but he assured them that he now enjoyed this pudding as much as he had previously relished succulent joints. On rare occasions Thomas might be prevailed upon to eat a few potatoes or a little boiled cabbage with the pudding, but nothing so pernicious as a dab of butter or a sprinkling of salt was allowed to come anywhere near them.

By 1770 stories of Thomas Wood's miraculous loss of weight and return to health had spread far and wide. Visitors came to Billericay specially to meet this remarkable man, and people from all over the world wrote to him asking for advice on how to slim. Wood was only too delighted to help others engaged in what he termed 'abstemious warfare' and spent hours every day composing letters of encouragement. His recommendations were always the same: 'Eat sparingly of plain food. Avoid fermented liquors, relishings, salt meats and sauces. Take regular exercise.'

Unfortunately few people had the will power to continue dieting for long, and after a week or so most of Wood's disciples fell by the wayside. He took an immense amount of trouble with those who did persevere, however, even visiting them in their homes to have a friendly chat. Further to strengthen the resolution of these slimmers, Thomas sent them little moral tales which described in ghastly detail the deaths of fat men who had given up their diets

Several society ladies, members of Parliament, lawyers, doctors and Indan nabobs recovered health and figure through following Wood's advice and all sent him tokens of their esteem. But his most fervent admirer was a Mr Buckle of Tewkesbury, who lost fifteen stone in two years and ended his final letter to Wood by saying: 'A picture of you will hang ever on my walls.'

As well as writing his own letters and visiting patients, Thomas Wood supervised the running of his two windmills. These were situated on a hill just outside Billericay, and to prevent anyone else from building a mill in the area Thomas planted elm trees in all the surrounding fields. At holiday times he used to put on pyrotechnic displays between the mills for the amusement of his friends.

No matter what else he did Thomas always managed to get in a few hours gardening every day. He loved flowers and was never seen without a nosegay in his button-hole. He also loved wild birds, and, sensing his affection, they were completely tame with him, eating out of his hands and perching on his head and shoulders.

In 1782 Mr Wood was as lean and fit as a boy. True his eyesight was beginning to fail, but his hearing was excellent and his appetite for pudding remained undiminished. He slept well and enjoyed great peace of mind. He hoped, therefore, that, like Cornaro, he would live to be a hundred. But fate decreed otherwise. On the

3. The wager between Mr Codd and Mr Hants of Maldon, for which seven "hundred" men (inhabitants of the Dengie Hundred) were buttoned into Edward Bright's waistcoat.

evening of May 20th, 1783, when he was sixty-three, the miller was suddenly taken ill. Next morning he was dead. He lies buried with other members of his family in Great Burstead churchyard.

Edward Bright, a contemporary of Wood, was born at Maldon on March 1st, 1721. He was descended on his mother's side from the Parliamentary major-general, John Desborough, who married Oliver Cromwell's sister, Jane, but his parents were not rich, and after a brief period at school, he began work as a post-boy, riding to Chelmsford and back every day.

This galloping about gave Edward a keep appetite, and when he returned home in the evenings he gorged himself on platefuls of stodgy food. By the time he was eleven he weighed ten stone, but he remained surprisingly quick and nifty. At twelve he left the postal service and was apprenticed to a Mr Pattison 'to learn the art of a grocer'.

Some ten years later we find Edward Bright running his own grocer's and tallow-chandler's shop in premises in Maldon High Street, now known as Church House. He and his wife and children lived above the shop. Edward was still eating gargantuan meals and he had developed a taste for old, strong beer. At twenty-two he weighed thirty stone.

Until he was twenty-six, Mr Bright rode to London once a week on business, and it is recorded that as he went along the streets his huge bulk was 'the gazing-stock and admiration of all people'. After he reached that age, however, his corpulence so taxed his strength that he could walk only a few yards and found even mounting a horse too much of an effort.

In 1749, when he was twenty-eight, Bright tipped the scales at forty-one stone. He continued to eat voraciously and drank a gallon of small beer and half a pint of wine per day. Up to this date his general health had been good, but now extreme shortness of breath kept him at home and on several occasions he suffered from fever and inflammation of the legs. Each time Bright fell ill his doctor would bleed him of two pints of blood and after that he usually recovered. But when at the end of October, 1750, he contracted typhus neither bleeding nor any other remedy availed, and by November 10th he was dead.

At the time of his death Edward Bright was a veritable mountain of a man, measuring 6ft. 11in. round the belly, 2ft. 8in. round the middle of his legs; and 2ft. 2in. round the middle of his arms. He was 5ft. 9in. tall and weighed just under forty-four stone. To accommodate this vast body a coffin 6ft. 7in. long; 3ft. 6in. wide;

and 3ft. deep was hurriedly put together, for although it was very cold the corpse putrefied at once and became offensive.

Moving the coffin from Bright's bedroom to the shop below was no easy task, and in the end a way had to be cut through the wall and staircase. A large crowd of relatives, friends and curious hangers-on attended the funeral, which took place on November 12th. The body was drawn on a carriage to All Saints church, Maldon, and was then lowered into a vault near the tower arch by means of a triangle and pulleys.

The entry on Bright in the parish register tells us that he was 'a very honest tradesman, a facetious companion, comely in his person, affable in his temper, a kind husband, a tender father and a valuable friend'. But the country as a whole cared little for his good qualities and merely regarded him as an interesting phenomenon. Artists, newsmongers and print-sellers were quick to spot his potential, and calling him 'The Great Bright' they made him out to be first the largest man in England, then the largest in Europe and finally in the world. Until 1809, when Daniel Lambert of Leicester died weighing fifty-two stone, Bright was in fact the heaviest Englishman of whom authentic record existed, and even after he lost his claim to that title he was long remembered as a minor national figure.

Perhaps what fixed Edward Bright so firmly in the minds of the populace was the famous 'bett' between two local shopkeepers, Mr Codd and Mr Hants, which was decided at the 'Black Bull', Maldon, on December 1st, 1750. One of these gentlemen maintained that he could button five hundred men into Bright's green baize waistcoat 'without breaking a single stitch'. The other declared it was impossible. When the matter came to trial, not five but seven 'hundred' men (inhabitants of the Dengie Hundred) were comfortably done up together inside the waistcoat. And if Bright had lived a little longer several more hundred men might have been included, for at the time of his death he had outgrown the waistcoat and was on the point of sending it to the tailor's to be let out.

Chapter Nine

POSTHUMOUS FAME

In June, 1752, the body of a young Essex beauty named Kitty was embalmed at Verona. In July the body was brought to England in a chest, and by August the strange tale attached to the corpse had become headline news.

Kitty was the daughter of Robert Canham, a tenant-farmer who lived at Beaumont Hall, near Thorpe-le-Soken. Here she was born on February 11th, 1720. As a child she was a bright, vivacious little thing; always gay, always laughing, very pretty. By her mid-teens she had become the toast of the neighbourhood, and as her father was a wealthy man suitors abounded. But Kate refused them all. She was enjoying herself immensely as a single woman and saw no reason why she should marry.

So with flirting and dancing and kindred amusements the years slipped by. Kitty's twenty-fifth birthday came and went and still she showed no signs of settling down. Her parents were getting anxious. They feared that despite her beauty their daughter would end up on the shelf, and they resolved that she should be forced to marry the next eligible man who offered for her.

This turned out to be Mr Alexander Gough, the new vicar of Thorpe-le-Soken. He began paying his addresses to Kate in the spring of 1745, and so effectively did the girl's parents nag at her that by the summer she had become engaged to him. She was not at all in love with Mr Gough, but she thought that by marrying him she might at least have a chance of happiness. Whereas she knew that if she stayed at home her parents' bitter reproaches would be unbearable. So she accepted Alexander. The wedding took place in the autumn of 1745, and after a brief honeymoon the couple returned to Thorpe.

It soon became clear to Kate that her bid for happiness was a failure. Mr Gough proved to be a scholarly man who disliked entertaining or going out much in society, and he would not allow his wife to go gadding about by herself. Occasionally, driven frantic by the monotonous vicarage routine, Kate defied her husband and went to a party or a ball, but when she came home he would yell abuse at her and fly into one of his terrible rages.

Life to Kitty was now a prison against whose bars she desperately beat her butterfly wings. She craved pleasure, excitement, admiration, and denied these suns of her existence she grew more and more depressed. Finally she could bear it no longer. In 1748 she left Mr Gough and fled to London.

Here Kate was in her element. Her dazzling beauty caused quite a sensation in the assembly rooms and she was surrounded by admirers. John, Viscount Dalmeny, eldest son of the second Earl of Rosebery was particularly attentive. He told Kate that he had been brought up in Italy and recounted wonderful stories about his travels and adventures. She was fascinated by him, and the pair quickly became friends. When later their friendship deepened into love and Lord Dalmeny asked Kitty to marry him, the temptation was too great. Without telling him that she was married already she became his bride.

After the ceremony the newly-weds went to Europe and spent four idyllic years leisurely touring the Continent. In 1752 the couple reached Verona. They did not have long to enjoy the beauties of this city, however, for within a month of their arrival Kate had contracted a fatal illness and was on her death-bed.

Just before she died Kitty confessed to her second husband that their marriage was bigamous and begged him to forgive her. She also asked him to take her body to England and see that it was buried in the churchyard at Thorpe. Half out of his mind with grief at the prospect of losing her, John forgave Kate at once and promised to do as she wished.

After her death he had her body embalmed and placed in a 'very handsome coffin with six large silver plates'. This he locked into a wooden chest. He then travelled across France with his sad burden and embarked with it on a ship bound for Dover. Once there he hired a small boat to convey him to Harwich. As the vessel was sailing up the East Coast a storm came on and the captain decided that it would be safer to go into the Colne and anchor at the Hythe at Colchester.

The customs men at the Hythe were extremely vigilant and as soon as they spotted the boat they came alongside to inspect the cargo. Not wishing to disclose his true identity Lord Dalmeny gave his name as Williams and declared that he was a Hamburg merchant in England on business. This did not satisfy the revenue officers, however, and they ordered all his boxes to be searched.

The first trunks that were opened contained jewellery and many fine silk dresses, frothy with lace. Instantly the men's suspicions were aroused. Smuggled goods. And when Lord Dalmeny refused to let them open the last and largest of his trunks their suspicions grew. One of the customs officers approached the chest with drawn sword, intending to run the blade through the wood—at that time the normal method of ascertaining the contents. Horrified, Dalmeny caught hold of the man and yelled at him to stop. The chest, he avowed, contained the body of his dearly beloved wife. At once it was forced open, and there indeed lay a beautiful woman.

Convinced now that the so-called merchant was in fact a murderer, the revenue men took the trunk to St. Leonard's church on Hythe Hill and, for want of a better prison, locked Lord Dalmeny in the vestry with it.

On the following day members of the public were allowed into the vestry for the purpose of identifying the corpse. And amongst those who visited the church was a gentleman who did recognise Kate. He questioned Dalmeny and managed to extract the true story from him.

Mr Gough was summoned to Colchester, and after seeing the corpse, he told the authorities that it was quite definitely that of his long lost wife. At first he was furious with Lord Dalmeny and threatened to kill him, but later, realising that the bigamous marriage was not the young man's fault, he grew more amicable.

On July 9th, 1752, Kitty's body was conveyed to Thorpe on a magnificent hearse drawn by six beplumed horses. Mutes in black silk hats rode behind. She was buried in a vault under the main aisle of Thorpe church, and the two husbands followed the coffin arm-in-arm, jointly mourning the lovely but capricious woman who had led them both such a dance.

The relatives of Sir Gilbert East were led a merry dance by their defunct kinsman, for when his will was read out after his death on December 11th, 1828, the directions for his funeral were found to be incredibly intricate and weird.

Sir Gilbert came from a prominent Berkshire family, but he owned the tithes of Witham, had a great affection for the place and wished to be buried there in the family vault beneath the church of St. Nicholas. Not in any old twopenny-halfpenny coffin, however. His relatives were to order a special cedar-wood coffin lined with Russian leather and half-filled with camphor and spices.

Into this Sir Gilbert's body was to be placed, and the whole was then to be sealed up and put into a wrought-iron coffin painted with six layers of black paint and 'embellished with armorial and funereal devices richly'. This outer coffin was to lie next to that of his wife and the two were to be encircled by a band of brass inscribed with the words: 'Whom God has joined together let no man put asunder'.

All these injunctions were faithfully carried out, and the elaborate funeral celebrations lasted for almost a week, much to the wonder of the inhabitants of Witham. Unfortunately, in the general excitement, one of Sir Gilbert East's express wishes was overlooked. This was that he should be 'buried in woollen'. So, after only a few days, the band was broken to enable his corpse to be dressed in a woollen suit. When this had been done the band was welded together again and the pair were allowed to rest in peace.

John Selletto of Brightlingsea did not believe in God, but just before he died in 1771, he made a vow to the effect that if he found there was a deity in the next world he would make a tree grow out of his grave. After his death he was buried near the south door of the parish church in a fine altar-tomb, and the vow was forgotten. But some years later a sapling forced its way through the stone, almost splitting the tomb in half.

The story of the vow was revived, and until the middle of the nineteenth century visitors came from miles around to see the tree growing from the 'Atheist's Tomb'. About that time it became unsafe and had to be chopped down. Legend has it that the tree was of an unknown, heavenly species, but it is far more likely that some joker put a seed into the earth beneath Selletto's coffin and that the tree was a perfectly ordinary oak or elm.

When Mrs Ruth Marriage, a Quakeress of Partridge Green Farm, Broomfield, died in 1772, she requested that her body should be buried under her favourite apple-tree in the orchard. Here she used to sit and meditate on sunny afternoons, and she thought that her spirit would be more at peace in this spot than in a churchyard.

Mrs Marriage was a widow for the last thirty-four years of her life, and for much of that time she acted as overseer of Broomfield parish. She was a wealthy and generous woman and always kept a store of ready money in the house to give to those in need. Once when part of the farmhouse caught fire she and her maids lowered the coins to the ground in buckets. And on another occasion these valiant females routed members of the Thaxted gang who had come to rob them.

For almost a century Ruth Marriage's grave was marked by a plain flat stone, but in 1857 one of her descendants, William Marriage, erected a brick tomb in her memory. This appears on large-scale Ordnance Survey maps as 'Vault'. Nowadays the tomb stands beside a hedge bounding a windswept field. The orchard with its original apple-tree disappeared long ago, but in about 1903 a new apple-tree was planted, the branches of which still spread protectingly over the tomb.

At Layer-de-la-Haye a grave on the extreme edge of St. John's churchyard is often pointed out to visitors. It belongs to a farmer who particularly loved the adjacent field and wished to be buried near it so that after death he could continue to hear sheep munching the grass.

As a boy Jeremy Bentham loved fields, especially the fields round Barking, where his father had a country house. Born in London in 1748, Jeremy was a weak sickly baby, and it was thought that the air of Barking would be good for him. So throughout his childhood he spent long periods there, with his paternal grandmother acting as nurse. Flowers were his delight when a lad and he would roam the fields gathering armfuls of wild blooms. But he liked wallflowers best and in old age wrote: 'So long as I retained my smell, a wallflower was a memento of Barking, and brought youth to my mind; for the wallflowers covered the walls, with their roots between the bricks'.

Life at Barking was 'paradise' to young Jeremy. He had gooseberry pie for supper every night, spent his days building cardhouses and his evenings playing 'ghosts' with the servants. He was very precocious and at the age of three his favourite treat was to be allowed to read Rapin's *History of England*. When he was eight Jeremy went to Westminster School, and at twelve he entered Queen's College, Cambridge. He obtained his B.A. degree at fifteen; his M.A. at nineteen.

Bentham's father then wished him to read law, and he did so to please the old man, but he disliked the profession and never practised. Instead he applied himself to the study of human affairs, trying to work out what is most conducive to the happiness of the greatest number and what opposed to it. His books and pamphlets on this and allied subjects soon won him universal acclaim, and he had a large following both in England and on the Continent.

When his father died in 1792, Jeremy Bentham inherited property in Essex and London and he moved into the elegant Hermitage in Queen Square, Westminster, where he remained for the rest of his life. In 1805 he proposed to Caroline Fox, Lord Holland's sister, but was rejected. From that time he shunned society and led a quiet bachelor existence.

Every day Bentham worked for about ten hours without stopping. On his desk there was always a canister of hot-spiced ginger nuts and a cup of coffee, which it was the duty of one of the servants to replenish at frequent intervals. Any friends Bentham wanted to see were invited to dine with him at seven o'clock, and after dinner the talk would continue fast and furious until the early hours of the morning. Such liberal-minded reformers as Sir Samuel Romilly, Lord Brougham, James Mill, Daniel O'Connell and Pierre Dumont were habitués at these gatherings.

Although often ill as a boy, Jeremy Bentham enjoyed robust health in manhood and old age, and when he was in his eighties he looked no more than sixty. He kept fit by eating simple food and trotting briskly round his garden once a day. On these runs he wore a long grey coat that flapped about his legs and a shapeless straw hat.

For the last two years of his life Bentham was engaged on a pamphlet entitled *Auto-Icon, or the Further Uses of the Dead to the Living*. In this curious piece of whimsy he puts forward the view that all dead bodies should be given for anatomical purposes to help doctors obtain a sounder knowledge of disease, but that the heads could be preserved by embalming. Churchyard space would thus be saved, he argues, for the heads could be kept at home, 'many generations being deposited on a few shelves in a moderate-sized cupboard'. Famous people could have their heads attached to a skeleton frame to make a full-sized auto-icon, and this would do away with the need for statues. Members of the nobility might even have auto-icons of their ancestors alternating with trees in their avenues.

In his will Jeremy Bentham bequeathed his own body to his physician, Thomas Southwood Smith, and requested that after dissection the head should be fixed to his skeleton, which was to be dressed in his customary apparel and placed in a glass case. When he died in 1832, at the age of eighty-four, these instructions were duly carried out, except that a wax head replaced Bentham's, as his face had lost all expression during the embalming process.

Dr Southwood Smith kept his former illustrious patient in his consulting rooms until his retirement in 1850. In that year, at Lord

Brougham's suggestion, Bentham was moved to University College, London, where he can still be seen today. Seated in his case in the cloisters, with his straw hat on his head and his favourite stick 'Dapple' in his hand, he looks as if he has come to pay a social call and will be getting up any minute to hurry back to his book-strewn desk at the Hermitage, his cup of coffee and canister of hot-spiced ginger nuts.

Chapter Ten

FINALE

Let us end with a medley of frolicsome beings; a rout of dwarfs and dreamers, lovers and fools. And who better to open the festivities than Mr Daniel Day, that benign bachelor of Wapping.

Daniel was born in 1683. He became a successful block and pump maker, and in 1720 invested in property around Hainault. This genial fellow could not bear the thought that rent-day should be a time of gloom for his tenants, however, and hit upon the splendid plan of inviting some of his friends along and turning the event into a festival. The giant Fairlop Oak in Hainault Forest seemed the ideal rendezvous for such a revel, and Day ordered his tenants to meet him under the branches of this tree on the first Friday in every July.

Here a picnic of bacon, beans and beer would be spread out on the grass, and as soon as business was concluded Daniel and his friends and tenants sat down to enjoy the feast. There was always much jollity and laughter at these gatherings. Fiddlers played, songs were sung and after the meal there would be dancing.

In 1725 a touch of pageantry was added to the festival when Day and his companions travelled from Wapping to Hainault in three fully-rigged model ships built onto coach frames, each drawn by six horses and attended by postilions dressed in blue and gold liveries. Musicians played on board the boats throughout the journey. Mr Day used this novel form of transport because, returning home after the previous year's junketing, he had met with a serious road accident, and had vowed that he would never again travel to the forest in a carriage.

The arrival of the boats at Fairlop was greeted by the tenants with such delight that Day resolved to include them as a permanent part of the festivities. As time went on, more and more of his friends wished to accompany him to Hainault, and extra ships were added to the fleet. These gaily painted craft attracted huge

75

crowds as they passed through Barking, Ilford and Fulwell Hatch, and uninvited guests began to follow the procession and join in the feasts. Daniel did not mind the intruders a bit. Sporting a sky-blue waistcoat and embroidered knee-breeches he stood in the hollow trunk of the Fairlop Oak, handing out panfuls of bacon and beans to all who came for them.

The eleven branches of this oak covered an area three hundred feet in circumference, and in the 1730s booths selling toys, ribbons and gingerbread were set up under the tree on the day of the festival. Later puppet-shows and fortune-tellers made their appearance. By the 1750s people from all parts of Essex and from London were coming to the festival, which was now generally known as the Fairlop Fair, and Daniel rejoiced at the merrymaking that went on around him, for there was nothing he liked better than seeing his fellow creatures happy.

One rent-day a massive bough was ripped from the Fairlop Oak in a gale, and Daniel ordered a coffin to be made out of the wood, as he believed the falling of the branch presaged his own death. When the coffin was ready he lay down in it to see if it was long enough, and found that it was a few inches too short. 'Never mind', he told the carpenter, 'you must desire my executors to cut off my head and put it between my legs.'

Despite the omen, Mr Day lived on for several more years, attended by a devoted housekeeper. This lady was inordinately fond of tea, and when she died, a short while before her master, he placed a packet of the favoured beverage in each of her hands prior to burial.

In 1767 Daniel Day was himself buried in his chosen coffin at Barking. He was long remembered in the Hainault area, for although the Fairlop Oak was destroyed in 1820, the festival he had created went on until July, 1899. And before the last group of revellers dispersed, a toast was proposed and solemnly drunk to the spirit of this kindly man.

In the latter half of the nineteenth century haymaking time was much looked forward to by the children of Woodford, for it was at this season of the year that a glorious gathering known as the 'Hares' Egg Tea-Party' took place. Mrs Richenda Barclay, wife of Alderman Henry Ford Barclay, who owned Monkhams House, Woodford, was the originator of this celebration, and to it she invited all the youngsters of the neighbourhood. They spent a wonderful afternoon hunting amongst the haycocks for 'hares' eggs', brightly coloured Easter eggs, that Mrs Barclay had hidden

Facing: 4. The Fairlop Fair, c. 1800.

there. They were then entertained to a lavish tea, and afterwards there were games, pony rides and a display of conjuring.

Another annual summer treat given by Mrs Barclay was for poor foreigners in London. Hundreds of Italian organ-grinders, French onion sellers and penniless Spaniards and Germans were brought to Woodford in charabancs, and spent a peaceful day wandering about the grounds of Monkhams. A vast quantity of food and drink was laid out in a marquee on the lawn, and the foreigners just helped themselves. In the evening they were given gifts and money before being driven back to London.

Mrs Barclay's generosity extended to animals as well as humans. Her house was a refuge for stray cats and dogs, which were allowed to wander freely in all the rooms, as were her own pet guinea pigs and tame hares. Once when she was on her way to Tottenham hospital Mrs Barclay noticed a horse without food in the pound at Tottenham Hale, and jumping out of her carriage, she waited by the roadside until a hay cart came by. She stopped the cart, bought a bale of hay, and only after she had seen the horse begin its meal did she continue her journey. Another time, at a formal dinner, she startled her sedate hostess by opening a window to admit a cat she had hear mewing outside and feeding the animal choice titbits from her plate.

Even more fond of animals was Miss Elizabeth Balls, who lived on the green at Havering-atte-Bower from 1785 to 1823. She entirely filled her cottage with chickens, sheep, cats, dogs and a number of specially beloved white goats whom she referred to as her 'dear children'.

In 1815 her family consisted of fourteen goats, two sheep, seventeen chickens, a cat and a poodle. The previous year she had possessed thirty-two goats, and it is recorded that at one time she had fifty of these creatures under her roof. Surrounded by animals, Miss Balls ate, slept and read her Bible. She rarely went out of the cottage, and never let anyone into it, except twice a year, when a man came to clear away the accumulated filth of the past six months.

In a shed beside her cottage Elizabeth Balls kept a pony and trap, and once a week she would drive into Romford to purchase hay for the goats. With her squinty eyes, dishevelled grey hair and ragged clothes she looked rather like a witch, and children were terrified of her. But they had no reason to be, for she was a gentle, kindly woman, always soft-spoken and polite.

Elizabeth's father had been a respectable farmer in Hemel Hempstead, where she was born, and for the first twenty-five years of her life she remained contentedly at home. But then came a tragic love affair. Miss Balls was jilted by her sweetheart, and, turning her back on human society for ever, she retired to Havering, where she began taking in animals to ease the loneliness of her solitary existence.

Two brothers who also renounced society were the Davies twins, fishermen from Alresford. In the 1880s and 90s these brothers lived all week on their smack *Odd Times*, and spent every Sunday at home with their sister. On Saturdays they put in at Brightlingsea to sell the fish they had caught and buy provisions for the next week's trip. Then they would go on a pub crawl round the town. They were both short, slight men, with wizened faces and piercing blue eyes. And as they walked along one behind the other, dressed identically in thick pilot-cloth trousers and Shetland jerseys, their shoulder-length hair and flowing beards precisely similar, they presented a curious sort of double vision, which provoked the laughter of all who saw them.

In the bars the brothers were taunted unmercifully, and one Saturday night, unable to bear the gibes of a particularly malicious scoffer, one of the twins drew a knife and stabbed the fellow in the chest. He was had up for attempted murder, found guilty and imprisoned. The remaining twin, completely helpless without his brother, pined away on board the fishing smack until, seeing his predicament, some townsfolk obtained the prisoner's release.

United once more, the Davies twins decided to opt out of a world that seemed to them so heartlessly cruel. They bade farewell to their sister, loaded their boat with equipment and set sail for the Dengie Flats, bleak stretches of marsh and mud lying between the mouths of the Blackwater and the Crouch. Here they spent the remainder of their days, living off fish, crabs and wild birds; only coming in contact with civilisation when they needed to replenish their barrels of water and beer.

William Kempe, of Spain's Hall, Finchingfield, withdrew not his person but his voice from the world. In 1588, when he was thirty-three, this squire married Philippa Gunter, daughter of a Hertfordshire gentleman. For a long while all was peace and harmony between them, and then suddenly in June, 1621, William quarrelled with his wife and accused her of unfaithfulness. Afterwards he felt such remorse for what his tongue had uttered that he vowed he would keep silence for seven years. This he did, and to mark each year of his vow he constructed seven fish-ponds in the grounds of Spain's Hall. At the end of the specified time William celebrated his new freedom of speech by taking part in Sunday service at the parish church. The whole village turned out to hear him pray, but unfortunately Philippa was not able to do so. She had been dead for over five years.

One March night during the Elizabethan era, John Brand of Great Hallingbury was told by an angel that he had better kill himself rather than marry the widow he loved. This was not the first time John had seen the angel, for on the previous Christmas Eve it had shown him in a vision where buried treasure lay, and afterwards he had found the gold. So he took the advice seriously, and on a Monday morning tried to stab himself to death. Friends saved him on that occasion, but Brand did not give up. On Wednesday he put a sack over his head, jumped into a pond and was almost drowned. The following Sunday he ate rat poison, which caused him such hideous pain that he rushed to an oak beside his house and hanged himself with a halter. He was buried, appropriately enough, beneath the village Hangman's Oak.

A woman living at Rochford in 1790 had been obsessed for the past eighteen years by a vision of the priceless jewels that she believed lay hidden under a certain spot at Rochford Hall. In the end she plucked up courage and asked the tenant of the hall if she might dig in that place. He gave his permission, but told her that she would have to ask the lord of the manor, Sir James Tylney-Long, whether he would want a share of the gems if any were found.

When Sir James next visited Rochford Hall, the old crone was waiting, and as he rode over the ground where she wished to dig, she threw herself in his path and begged him to let her keep whatever she might find buried there. He granted her request and ordered his servant to help her in her search. After many hours digging they came upon a great stone, beneath which the woman said the gems were concealed. Alas, when the stone was taken up, no casket of jewels appeared, and she fainted from shock. To lessen her disappointment Sir James Tylney-Long gave her a handsome money present, and she finally went off home, well pleased with her treasure seeking.

From 1822 to 1824 another visionary, a Scotsman named Gregor MacGregor, was living at Oak Hall, Wanstead, as the guest of Major John Richardson. In the early part of 1821, while he was soldiering in the Caribbean, MacGregor had secured a land concession in Nicaragua. Calling this land 'The Sovereign State of

Poyais' and introducing himself as 'His Serene Highness Gregor I' he came to London soon afterwards to seek recognition and obtain funds to develop his country.

In the capital, MacGregor met Major Richardson, on whom he conferred an impressive number of titles. The major was charmed by this royal personage and insisted that he make Oak Hall his headquarters throughout his stay in England. For two years a constant stream of bankers, stockbrokers and important officials arrived at the house to attend State banquets and musical soirées. All the great Essex families came to call on Prince Gregor, and the Lord Mayor of London entertained him frequently when he was in town. By the autumn of 1824 MacGregor had appointed the ministers who were to govern in Poyais and had been advanced £200,000.

His Serene Highness was about to depart for his dominions when a few rather unfortunate facts came to light. It was discovered that the 'Kingdom of Poyais' consisted of two or three barren acres which had not even been paid for, and that its Prince had no right whatever to that title. The bonds he had presented to satisfy the financiers were found to be totally worthless, and he was apprehended and flung into prison for debt.

MacGregor's illusions of grandeur did not desert him in his hour of need, however, and by promising his gaolers various dukedoms and rewards he won their sympathy and was allowed to escape to France. He died in Caracas in 1845, still believing himself to be a great and powerful ruler.

Mr John Archer, of Coopersale, near Epping, was the exact oppo-site of MacGregor. He was a millionaire who owned a vast amount of land in Essex and was entitled to live like a prince. But he hid himself away in a tiny cottage and saw no one except his steward. He was estranged from his wife, and had quarrelled with his two daughters by a previous marriage. Nevertheless, when he died in 1800 he left property and an immense fortune to be divided up between his womenfolk. The mansion at Coopersale, which had not been lived in for many years, was inherited by one of the daughters, a Mrs Susannah Houblon, and after her father's funeral she paid a surveyor to go over the house and report his findings.

Three days later the man returned with a truly fantastic story. It appeared that when he reached Coopersale he found the gates and the front door of the house crumbling on their hinges. The court-yard was a matted tangle of thistles and briars, and the entrance hall was deep in dust. Pigeons had built their nests amongst the priceless books in the library, and in the drawing-room an owl was living in splendid isolation. Strands of cobweb hung down from every chandelier; some webs extended the whole length of a room. Flabbergasted by his discoveries the surveyor had gone to see the bailiff, and the old man had told him that no one had entered the mansion for about twenty-five years. His master had given strict orders that no work was to be done in the house or gardens; yet all the servants had received their regular wages.

No one knew exactly why John Archer should have wanted his ancestral home to fall into ruins. But his first wife, Mary, had died at Coopersale in 1776, after a long illness, and it was believed that he considered the mansion to have been in some obscure way responsible for her death, and had taken his revenge upon it by leaving it to rot.

At Gidea Hall, another famous Essex mansion, a dwarf in cap and bells danced nightly on chairs and table-tops throughout the 1580s. He was William Cooper, jester to the family of Richard Cooke, son of Sir Anthony Cooke, who tutored Edward VI. When the dwarf grew too old for such capers, his master granted him an annuity of £10, which he enjoyed until his death in August, 1616. He was buried at Romford, and is charmingly described in the parish register as 'Will Cooper—ye dwarfe of Giddie Hall'.

Going back in time to the reign of King Stephen, when dragons flew and giants stalked the earth, we come across two elfin children found at Woolpit, Suffolk, by the retainers of Sir Richard de Calne and brought as curiosities to his castle at Wix. The children, a brother and sister, looked just like human infants, except that their skin was bright green. They spoke a language none could understand.

When they arrived at Wix, Sir Richard offered them bread and meat, but they would not touch the food. It was later discovered that raw green beans were the only things the pair would eat, and they lived on these throughout the summer. The little boy died during the winter, but the girl became accustomed to a normal diet and gradually lost her green colour. She lived in Sir Richard's household for many years, and as soon as she had picked up enough English to make herself understood, she was questioned about her origin.

She said that she came from a land of perpetual twilight, where no sun ever rose or darkness fell. The inhabitants were all green, as were their plants, animals and possessions. Asked how she and her brother came to Suffolk, the girl replied that they had been tending sheep in their own world when they suddenly heard sweet music issuing from the mouth of a certain cavern. Lured on by the exquisite melodies they had wandered through the cave until they reached an entrance through which daylight was pouring. When they emerged into the sun's glare the unaccustomed brightness knocked them senseless, and in that state they had been found by Sir Richard's servants.

This story was written down by Ralph, Abbot of Coggeshall, a close friend of Sir Richard de Calne, and already in 1200, when he was living at Coggeshall, its inhabitants were acquiring that reputation for singularity which led to their being regarded as the most eccentric folk in Essex and put them on a par with the Men of Gotham.

Legend has it that the people of Coggeshall once tried to fish the moon out of the River Blackwater with hay-rakes, thinking it was a ball of gold, and that they put hurdles across the road to prevent the scarlet fever at Kelvedon from entering their town. These tales stuck, and in time any particularly ludicrous action, real or fictitious, came to be known locally as a 'Coggeshall job'.

Here are a few of the most amusing jobs that have been handed down over the centuries. Once when the Blackwater burst its banks and flooding seemed inevitable, a woman living in a house in Bridge Street, Coggeshall, cut away the bottom stairs to stop the water getting up to her bedroom. On another occasion a Coggeshall man who had to get up very early found that he had only one match with which to light his candle in the morning, so he struck it the previous night to make sure it was a good one. It was the people of Coggeshall who locked a wheelbarrow in a shed, fearing that it would go mad after having been bitten by a dog with rabies. And it was Coggeshall folk who once hoisted a cow up to the church tower, so that it could eat the grass they had seen growing from crevices in the brickwork. The Coggeshall Town Band was rehearsing in a house one morning when a friend came in and told the bandsmen how lovely the music sounded from the street. Immediately they put down their instruments and trooped out to listen.

But perhaps the best story is the one about the Coggeshall Volunteers who were being trained during the Napoleonic Wars. None of the men knew their left from their right, and drill practice was a nightmare to the sergeant until he thought of making them tie a wisp of hay to their left legs and a wisp of straw to their right legs, after which he had only to shout, 'Hay, straw! Hay, straw! Hay, straw!' to have them all marching along in perfect formation.

BIBLIOGRAPHY

Addison, William, *Epping Forest, Its Literary and Historical Associations*. London, 1947.

Addison, William, *Essex Heyday*. London, 1949.

Addison, William, *The English Country Parson*. London, 1947.

Andrews, William, *Bygone Essex*. London, 1892.

Angelo, Henry, *Reminiscences of*, 2 vols. London, 1828.

An Old Essex Correspondence—Letters to and from Thomas Wood, Miller of Billericay. Southend-on-Sea, 1923.

Aveling, J. H., *The Chamberlens and the Midwifery Forceps*. London, 1882.

Barns, Stephen J., 'Aaron Hill and his Father-in-law, Edmund Morris'. *Essex Review*, April, 1934.

Barrett, C. R. B., *Essex, Highways, Byways and Waterways*. 1892.

Barrett-Lennard, T., *An Account of the Families of Lennard and Barrett*. 1908.

Baumgardt, David, *Bentham and the Ethics of Today*. Princetown University Press, 1952.

Bax, Clifford, *Highways and Byways in Essex*. London, 1939.

Beer, E. S. de (ed.), *The Diary of John Evelyn*. London, 1959.

Benham, W. G. *Essex Sokens*. Colchester, 1928.

Bensusan, S. L., *A Countryside Chronicle*. London, 1907.

Bentham, Jeremy, *Auto-Icon, or the Further Uses of the Dead to the Living*. 1842.

Benton, Philip, *The History of the Rochford Hundred*, 2 vols. 1867.

Blackman, John, *A Memoir of the Life and Writings of Thomas Day*, London, 1862

Bosworth, George F., *Essex Past and Present*. London, 1898.

Brown, Herbert, *A History of Bradwell-on-Sea*. Chelmsford, 1929.

Burdon, H., 'The Waltham Blacks'. *Essex Review*, January, 1904.

Burke's *Landed Gentry*. 1863.

Cambridge Journal, August 15th, 1752.

Caunt, George, *Essex Blood and Thunder*. 1967.

Cavendish, Margaret, Duchess of Newcastle, *Grounds of Natural Philosophy*. London, 1668; *Nature's Pictures*. London, 1656; *Playes*. London, 1662; *Poems and Fancies*. London, 1653; *Sociable Letters*. London, 1664; *The Life of the Thrice Noble, High and Puissant Prince, William Cavendish*. London, 1667; *The World's Olio*. London, 1665.

Chelmsford Quarter-Sessions rolls, December, 1581.

Christy, Miller, 'A Lonely Grave at Broomfield'. *Essex Review*. April, 1903.

Clark, Charles, *John Noakes and Mary Styles, or an Essex Calf's Visit to Tiptree Races*. London, 1839; *Metrical Mirth about Marriageable Misses, or the Modern Mode in Matters Matrimonial*. Great Totham Press, 1848; *Mirth and Mocking on Sinner-Stocking* (Broadside 1). Great Totham Press; *Mirth and Mocking on Sinner-Stocking* (Broadsides 2 and 3). Essex Standard Office, Colchester; *Tiptree Fair*. Great Totham Press, 1844; *Tiptree Races*. London, 1834.

Collection of British Poets—The Poems of Aaron Hill. Chiswick, 1822.

Coller, D. W., *The People's History of Essex*. Meggy and Chalk, Chelmsford, 1861.

Cornaro, Luigi, *Discourses on a Sober and Temperate Life*. London, 1768.

Crespigny, Sir Claude Champion de, *Forty Years of a Sportsman's Life*. Mills and Boon Ltd., London, 1910.

Cromwell, Thomas, *The History of the Ancient Town of Colchester*, 2 vols. London, 1825.

Crook, G. T. and Rayner, J. L., *The Complete Newgate Calendar*, 5 vols. London, 1926.

Dewar, George A. B., (ed.) *Sporting Memoirs of Sir Claude de Crespigny*. Lawrence and Bullen Ltd., London, 1897.

Dickin, E. P., *A History of the Town of Brightlingsea*. Colchester, 1939.

Dictionary of National Biography.

Dodgson, Campbell, 'An English Engraver of the Restoration'. *The Connoisseur*, Vol. 1. 1901.

Essex Leaders—Social and Political. William Pollard and Co., Exeter, 1895.

Essex Standard, March 9th, 1849.

Fitch, E. A., *Maldon and the River Blackwater*. 1898.

Gentleman's Magazine, December, 1789; February, 1793; June, 1794; January, 1824; March, 1824.

Glenny, W. W., 'Jeremy Bentham'. *Essex Review*, October, 1896.

Goulding, Richard W., *Margaret Lucas—Duchess of Newcastle*. Lincolnshire Chronicle Ltd., Lincoln, 1925.

Great Hallingbury Church Wardens' Accounts (1538-1630).

Harriott, John, *Struggles Through Life*, 3 vols. London, 1815.

Hickeringill, Edmund, *Works*, 2 vols. London, 1716.

Hill, Aaron, *An Account of the Rise and Progress of the Beech-Oil Invention*. London, 1715.

Hill, Aaron, *Four Essays*. London, 1718.

Hope, Moncrieff, A. R., *Essex*. A. C. Black Ltd., London, 1926.

Houblon, Lady A. Archer, *The Houblon Family, Its Story and Times*, 2 vols. A. Constable and Co. Ltd., 1907.

Keir, James, *An Account of the Life and Writings of Thomas Day*. London, 1791.

King, H. W., *Ecclesiae Essexienses*, 5 vols. Unpublished MS. belonging to the Essex Record Office.

Knights, Edward S., *Essex Folk*. Heath Cranton Ltd., London, 1935.

London Gazette, November 29th, 1703.

London Evening Post, August 15th, 1752.

Majdalany, Fred, *The Red Rocks of Eddystone*. Longmans Ltd., London, 1959.

Maldon Parish Registers.

Mason, Mrs C., *Essex, Its Forest, Folk and Folklore*. J. H. Clarke and Co., Chelmsford, 1928.

Mee, Arthur, *Essex*. Hodder and Stoughton Ltd., London, 1942.

Morant, Philip, *The History and Antiquities of Essex*, 2 vols. London, 1816.

Newman, L. G., *A History of Great Bentley*. 1960.

Ogborne, Elizabeth, *A History of Essex*. London, 1814.

Redding, Cyrus, *Memoirs of Remarkable Misers*, 2 vols. 1863.

Roe, Fred, *Essex Survivals*. Methuen and Co. Ltd., London, 1929.

Sadler, Sir Michael, *Thomas Day—An English Disciple of Rousseau*. Cambridge University Press, 1928.

Saffron Walden Parish Registers.

Seward, Anna, *Memoirs of the Life of Dr. Darwin*. London, 1804.

Sitwell, Dame Edith, *English Eccentrics*. Faber and Faber Ltd., London, 1933.

Smith, Rev. Harold, *Ecclesiastical History of Essex Under the Long Parliament and the Commonwealth*. Benham and Co. Ltd., Colchester.

Solly, Lt.-Col. A. R., 'Edmund Hickeringill, Eccentric'. *Essex Review*, July, 1949.

Southwood Smith, T., *A Lecture Delivered Over the Remains of Jeremy Bentham Esquire in the Webb Street School of Anatomy and Medicine on June 9th, 1832*.

Sprigge, Timothy L. S., (ed.) *The Correspondence of Jeremy Bentham*, Vols. 1 and 2, Athlone Press, 1968.

Swallow, William, *Medical Notebook*. (B. M. Sloane MS. 1529.)

The Spectator, May 19th, 1712.

Thompson, J. O., (ed.) *Dr. Salter: Diary and Reminiscences 1849-1932*. The Bodley Head Ltd., London, 1933.

Topham, Edward, *The Life of the Late John Elwes Esquire*, London, 1791.

Transactions of the College of Physicians, Vol. 2, 1771.

Trevelyan, Raleigh, *A Hermit Disclosed*. Longmans Ltd., London, 1960.

Turner, James, *The Dolphin's Skin—Six Studies in Eccentricity*. Cassell and Co. Ltd., London, 1956.

Vaughan, E., *These For Remembrance*. Benham and Co. Ltd., Colchester, 1934.

Warren, C. Henry, *Essex*. Robert Hale and Co., London, 1950.

Wheatley, Henry B., (ed.) *The Diary of Samuel Pepys*, Vols. 4-6, Bell and Sons Ltd., London, 1962.

White, John, *The First Century of Scandalous, Malignant Priests*. London, 1643.

Woolf, Virginia, *The Common Reader*, First and Second Series, The Hogarth Press Ltd., London, 1965.

Wright, Thomas, *A History of Essex*, 2 vols. London, 1831.

INDEX OF ESSEX CHARACTERS AND PLACES